0755:
THE HEROES OF
PEARL HARBOR

Donald K. &
Helen L. Ross

Other books by
Donald K. and Helen L. Ross
WASHINGTON STATE MEN OF VALOR
and by
Helen L. Ross
TOUCH OF SMILE
PASSPORT TO ISTANBUL

For additional copies of
"0755: PEARL HARBOR HEROES"
send $12.00 to

ROKALU PRESS
15871 Glenwood Road SW
Port Orchard WA 98366

Additional information and
corrections, when authenticated,
are welcome at same address.

Typography and printing in the USA by Sutherland Publishing
Inc., Montezuma, Iowa 50171.

ISBN 0-930942-15-9

Let us remember December 7th

as

a day of

MAGNIFICENT COURAGE!

DEDICATION

To all those swabbies, leathernecks,
ground pounders and airdales
who performed beyond the call of duty
on December 7, 1941
during the Japanese attack
at Pearl Harbor,
of whom many were never recognized
for their valiant efforts.

TABLE OF CONTENTS

ABOUT THE AUTHORS

The subject of Pearl Harbor is a natural one for this writing couple who experienced the Pearl Harbor attack first hand and have studied this topic for many decades.

Don Ross, native of Beverly, Kansas, and recipient of the Medal of Honor for action at Pearl Harbor, retired from the Navy as a Captain after 27 years. He is well acquainted with surviving Medal of Honor and other medal recipients. Captain Ross is a popular speaker on many historical subjects, with a nation-wide audience.

Helen, born in Chicago, Illinois, has been a productive writer since high-school days, is a National Federation of PEN WOMEN member and long-time Board member of Pacific Northwest Writers Conference. This is her fourth book (one co-authored with Don); a former AP correspondent, she served as Correspondent for TIME-LIFE's "ABOVE and BEYOND," a Medal of Honor history.

Buried in files, scrapbooks, letters and memories, information for this study required four years of research and travel. The book answers many questions about the immediate response of our fighting men at the beginning of World War Two.

FOREWORD

This volume by Don and Helen Ross provides all of us with a very special insight of America. It is a compendium of instances which addresses the spirit and soul of our Nation.

On July 9, 1987, pursuant to my duties as the Special Assistant Secretary of the Navy (Safety and Survivability), I stood on the deck of the **USS STARK** (FFG-31) at her berth in Mayport, Florida. My inspection completed, I was casually talking with personnel who had survived the Iraqi attack on their ship in the Persian Gulf on May 17th, 1987.

The feeling of deja vu was overwhelming. I was talking to young Americans who had heroically responded to a surprise attack on their ship. Their performance was so outstanding, that they had saved the only ship of its type ever struck by a cruise-type missile, much less two such missiles. Individuals whose training and experience would hardly suggest the quality of their reactions under stress, had exceeded any reasonable expectation of performance.

Their personal bravery had brought their ship through a tragic trial, just as so many of my contemporaries had done, some forty-six years before under similar surprise circumstances at Pearl Harbor.

Of a certainty, personnel of the Navy today are taller on the average than my shipmates on the **USS NEVADA** (BB-36) on December 7, 1941. They are far stronger...their high school contemporaries achieve track and field records which were World Records in 1941. They are far better educated, thanks to the GI Bill following World War II which stimulated our present educational system.

There was also no question in my mind, as my eye wandered to see the Stars and Stripes waving proudly on the stern flagstaff, that these young people had as much courage, fearlessness, and, yes, "guts," as my contemporaries of so many, many years ago.

Don and Helen Ross have provided a historical snapshot of why the flag of the United States of America will always fly proudly from the flagstaffs of our armed forces.

Young Americans, from Lexington and Concord to the **STARK** share the common heritage which has preserved us our Nation.

They are the reason our flags still flew after the Japanese broke off their attack on December 7, 1941, and still flies on **STARK.**

This is a very important volume, far beyond the concentration on a single battle. This is America in a capsule.

In its pages are individuals who came from every walk of life...every rung on the socio-economic ladder of the Nation. From the cities, farms, mountains, mines, prairies, and sea coasts.

Their common denominator is found in the simple phrase, "I am an American."

Here then, is our Nation in miniature...it is "We the People..." in the most important individual scenarios our citizens must face.

I am certain the authors will join me in recognizing that this work omits the names of literally hundreds of others who fought in the battle with Don and me. These individuals were not specifically recognized for their outstanding courage and bravery...often exceeding the performance of us whose conduct was recognized. To those who read this volume, I offer you my salute...the recognition of one warrior for another.

This is why we so often raise our voices in the song, "God Bless America."

Joseph K. Taussig, Jr.
Captain, U.S. Navy (Retired)

NOTE: Capt. Taussig, recipient of the Navy Cross (pp 50, 51) now serves as Assistant to the Secretary of the Navy.

INTRODUCTION

Almost every item in the shop centered on one subject—Pearl Harbor. And why not?

I stood in the **ARIZONA** Memorial Museum reception center at Pearl Harbor, surrounded by books, pamphlets, photos, tapes, souvenirs—all about the infamous attack of December 7, 1941.

Earlier in the day, while units assembled for a parade in Waikiki, a Fleet Reserve Chief Petty Officer approached me. He knew me as Historian for the Congressional Medal of Honor Society and co-author of a book on that subject.

Introducing himself as the Memorial Museum book store manager, he said, "Captain Ross, we have many volumes out there about Pearl Harbor and the ships but nothing about the heroes. Few people seem to know how many Medals of Honor were awarded or that hundreds of other men were highly decorated.

"The fact is," he continued, "people ask every day for information about heroes and medals awarded for that day. I have heard of no such book or listings. Do you happen to know of one?"

I didn't, but said I would do what I could about it.

Back on the Mainland, wife Helen and I started the long exciting search which swung from invigorating to infuriating. Using a scrapbook worn from 40 years of fingering, we pieced together names and citations for recipients of a dozen different medals, and lists of those receiving Letters of Commendation.

The twelve printed lines per inch in the war-news packed papers required page-size magnifiers and considerable eyestrain. In spite of this inconvenience, our knowledge grew daily as did our appreciation of the determination and courage of our fighting men on the war's first day.

Near the top of the alphabetized Medal of Honor list stands First Lieutenant George H. Cannon, United States Marine Corps, who performed courageously on the Island of Midway. Thus having stretched our research horizon beyond Pearl Harbor and Oahu, we excavated westward to Midway and beyond. Time also extended to include deeds performed as late as June 1942. In most instances the activities related in some way to Pearl Harbor, if only in that the decorating ceremony took place in the Harbor or on Oahu.

We hoped to complete our task through letters and phone calls to Washington, DC. Our expectations ended in shock and disappointment when informed that no list of heroes, except for Medal of Honor recipients, exists in any branch of the Armed Services. A standard reply from offices and commands was, "If you know the names, we can supply the Citations." A Catch 22 situation indeed.

Our continued study brought out the fact that awards are not the only benefit reaped from an attack such as Pearl Harbor. Medals, citations and material spoils of war become miniscule in value compared to spiritual and mental gain. Richard Fuchs said it best in EVEN DEATH PASSED THEM BY.[1]

"Medals are not awarded for victory in battle (but) for victory of the human spirit. . . . a medal honors triumph of endurance and courage over fear and over self often marking the fiery passage from youth to manhood."

Seasoned quickly in a few hours, 7 December veterans who exhibited ability and skill, moved out weeks and months later, into fleet and troops as leaders and instructors. Men who in peace would have marked time for advancement were able to leap the ladders of rates and ranks. Individuals in every Service branch experienced rapid maturity through immediate responsibility.

One of those so affected was Major Alan Shapley, U.S. Marine Corps. He received the Silver Star for his gallant performance, later retiring from the Corps as Lieutenant General topping a brilliant career.

Another was Gunner Jackson Pharris, USN who, for action at Pearl Harbor received the Navy Cross in 1942. Years later, this was upgraded to a Medal of Honor. He retired as a Lieutenant Commander.

Still another was Charles W. Davis, young infantry officer, US Army, stationed at Schofield Barracks 7 December. He advanced to Captain and by January 1943 served as Executive Officer of a battalion on Guadalcanal where he performed in a manner worthy of the Medal of Honor. He retired from the Army as a Colonel.

Lastly, the Army Air Corps proved to be a training ground for Edward S. Michael who retired as a Lieutenant Colonel. He was a Private stationed at Wheeler Field, awaiting transportation to Flight School on 7 December. Two years later, as First Lieutenant and pilot, he merited the Medal during a flight over Germany.

Like kernels of popcorn, moisture released to expand for glorious productivity, America's men—and women— responded to the heat of the day, often surpassing anyone's expectations. While ships and planes sank and burned, spirits of fighting men rose in defense and patriotism.

---

1. *Article published in VFW MAGAZINE February 1983.*

In addition to our military heroes we salute those hundreds of men and several women, civilian and military, who received Letters of Commendation from people in high places. Over 300 courageous individuals were so recognized by President Franklin Delano Roosevelt, Secretary of Navy Frank Knox, Commander-in-Chief Pacific Fleet Admiral Chester W. Nimitz or many other Commanding Officers.

Their deeds, spectacular in narration, horrifying in reality, include drilling and cutting through thick skins of ships, fighting against time to rescue trapped and suffocating men, battling gaseous and cordite fires hours on end, clearing debris and bodies from the burning surface of the Harbor's water. Such dedication to nauseating duty.

Many heads of departments and unit leaders remarked in essence, "I never can forget how every man was ready to perform his duty and someone else's if need be." For some, like Tennyson's hero, "The path of duty was the way to glory," while others performed unseen, unrecorded and unsung.

An editorial in THE HONOLULU ADVERTISER of April 3, 1942 caught my eye. It read in part, "If a corps of authors were to set themselves to write a book on each navy hero honored at Pearl Harbor this week, there would be a lifetime of writing ahead. Fourteen[1] Medals of Honor were awarded, 48 Navy Crosses and several hundred letters of commendation given to men who participated heroically. . .

"A book is no exaggeration." The editorial continues, "In those minutes and hours in which bombs tore at ships and machine guns spit bullets as of hail, men lived a lifetime; what each did and thought in the hell-drama of a Sunday morning is enough to rivet any reader to the pages of its account."

Most of the information for such a book was not available during the war and only many years later has much of it become accessible, and in many cases only after deep probing. Perhaps this is the golden moment for such a book.

We enlarged our geographical area beyond Pearl Harbor for several reasons. Courage and bravery were not limited to Pearl Harbor that Sunday, but were exhibited over much of the island of Oahu, at Wake, Midway and the Philippines. Also, we not only extended the area, but time, because many awards, though merited during later days and months, were finally awarded on ships in Pearl Harbor and on parade grounds at various Army Commands on Oahu.

---

1. *Two additional Medals of Honor were awarded after the April 1942 decorating ceremony at Pearl Harbor.*

Besides satisfying the interested reader about our heroes, we point out a second goal. Although we list only 249 medal recipients, our study definitely recognizes every man who performed his best during the many conflicts, as a hero. Without the men behind the recognized "heroes" there could be no defense, no retaliation, no unity of purpose to electrify the nation.

With this in mind, we salute not only our decorated men and women but all those who served faithfully and bravely on 7 December 1941 and the immediate following months of World War Two.

Medal of Honor

MEDAL OF HONOR

RULES GOVERNING THE AWARDING OF A MEDAL OF HONOR

Boards of Decorations for each Armed Service have set regulations which permit no margin of doubt or error in judging whether or not a man is entitled to the Medal of Honor. The criteria are:

The deed of the nominated person must be proved beyond any doubt by testimony of at least two eye-witnesses.

The deed must be so outstanding that it clearly distinguishes the nominee's gallantry beyond the call of duty from lesser forms of bravery.

It must involve the risk of life.

It must be the type of deed which, if it had not been done, it would not subject him to any justified criticism.[1]

DESCRIPTION

Originally, the Army and Navy used the same medal, a five-pointed star, designed at its inception, for the Navy in 1861 during the Civil War. Made of bronze, each point contains a branch of oak and laurel, terminating in a trefoil. In the center, encircled by thirty-four stars, America, personified as Minerva, her helmet bearing an eagle, stands with her left hand supporting fasces, while her right hand holds the United States shield with which she repulses Discord who holds two serpents in each hand. On the reverse is engraved the name, rank, and ship of the recipient, and the place and date of the deed for which Medal was given.

This design continued to be used by both services until 1904 when the Army requested an entirely new delineation. The chief feature of the old medal, a five-pointed star, has been retained; in its center appears the head of the heroic Minerva, the highest symbol of wisdom and righteous war. Surrounding this central feature in circular form are the words, "United States of America." An open laurel wreath, enameled in green, encircles the star, and the oak leaves at the bases of the prongs of the star are likewise enameled in green to give them prominence.

---

1. *U.S. Senate, MEDAL OF HONOR RECIPIENTS, 1863-1978, U.S. Gov't. Printing, Washington, D.C., 1978*

The Air Force created its own Medal in 1963. The design is similar to the Army Medal with the green enameled wreath. The head of the Statue of Liberty replaces Minerva and the ribbon attachment is ornate with bolts of lightning. At the time of the Pearl Harbor attack, heroes of Naval and Marine aviation received Navy Medals of Honor; and Army Air Corps flyers received the Army Medal of Honor.

MEDAL OF HONOR RECIPIENTS

*BENNION, Capt. Mervin S., U.S. NAVY
*CANNON, First Lt. George H., U.S. MARINE CORPS
 FINN, Chief Aviation Ordanceman John William, U.S. NAVY
*FLAHERTY, Ensign Frank C., U.S. NAVY
•FUQUA, Lt. Cmdr. Samuel Glenn, U.S. NAVY
*HILL, Chief Boatswain Edwin Joseph, U.S. NAVY
*JONES, Ensign Herbert Charpiot, U.S. NAVAL RESERVE
*KIDD, Rear Admiral Isaac C. Kidd, U.S. NAVY
•PHARRIS, Gunner Jackson Charles, U.S. NAVY
*REEVES, Chief Radioman Thomas J., U.S. NAVY
 ROSS, Machinist Donald K., U.S. NAVY
*SCOTT, Machinist Mate Robert R., U.S. NAVY
*TOMICH, Chief Watertender Peter, U.S. NAVY
*VAN VALKENBURG, Capt. Franklin, U.S. NAVY
*WARD, Seaman 1st Class James R., U.S. NAVY
•YOUNG, Cmdr. Cassin, U.S. NAVY

* Posthumous awards
•Deceased since Pearl Harbor

NOTE: The above rates and ranks are those held on 7 December 1941. The individual Citations were copied as printed in the 1978 U.S. Senate's MEDAL OF HONOR RECIPIENTS 1863-1978 where rates and ranks are often those of later dates. Therefore, headings and Citations will not agree for FINN, FUQUA and PHARRIS.

CITATIONS FOR MEDAL OF HONOR

*CAPTAIN MERVIN S. BENNION, USN

"Rank and organization: Captain, U.S. Navy. Born: 5 May 1887, Vernon, Utah. Appointed (to Naval Academy) from: Utah.

"Citation: For conspicuous devotion to duty, extraordinary courage, and complete disregard of his own life, above and beyond the call of duty, during the attack on the Fleet in Pearl Harbor, by Japanese forces on 7 December 1941. As Commanding Officer of the **USS WEST VIRGINIA,** after being mortally wounded, Capt. Bennion evidenced apparent concern only in fighting and saving his ship, and strongly protested against being carried from the bridge."

* Posthumous award

*FIRST LIEUTENANT GEORGE H. CANNON, U.S. MARINE CORPS

"Rank and organization: First Lieutenant, U.S. Marine Corps. Born: 5 November 1915, Webster Groves, Mo. Entered service at: Michigan.

"Citation: For distinguished conduct in the line of his profession, extraordinary courage and disregard of his own condition during the bombardment of Sand Island, Midway Islands, by Japanese forces on 7 December 1941. First Lieutenant Cannon, Battery Commander of Battery H, 6th Defense Battalion, Fleet Marine Force, U.S. Marine Corps, was at his command post when he was mortally wounded by enemy shellfire. He refused to be evacuated from his post until after his men who had been wounded by the same shell were evacuated, and directed the reorganization of his command post until forcibly removed. As a result of his utter disregard of his own condition he died from loss of blood."

* Posthumous award

NOTE: Appointed from Michigan, Cannon graduated from the Naval Academy.

CHIEF AVIATION ORDNANCEMAN JOHN WILLIAM FINN, U.S. NAVY

"Rank and organization: Lieutenant, U.S. Navy. Place and date: Naval Air Station, Kaneohe Bay, Territory of Hawaii, 7 December 1941. Entered service at: California. Born: 23★ July 1909, Los Angeles, Calif.

"Citation: For extraordinary heroism, distinguished service, and devotion above and beyond the call of duty. During the first attack by Japanese airplanes on the Naval Air Station, Kaneohe Bay on 7 December 1941, Lieutenant Finn, then Chief Aviation Ordnanceman, promptly secured and manned a .50 caliber machine gun mounted on an instruction stand in a completely exposed section of the parking ramp, which was under heavy enemy machine gun strafing fire. Although painfully wounded many times, he continued to man this gun and to return the enemy's fire vigorously and with telling effect throughout the enemy strafing and bombing attacks and with complete disregard for his own personal safety. It was only by specific orders that he was persuaded to leave his post to seek medical attention. Following first aid treatment, although obviously suffering much pain and moving with great difficulty, he returned to the squadron area and actively supervised the rearming of returning planes. His extraordinary heroism and conduct in this action were in keeping with the highest tradi-tions of the U.S. Naval Service."

★Finn corrects this to read 24 July 1909.

*ENSIGN FRANK C. FLAHERTY, USN

"Rank and organization: Ensign, U.S. Naval Reserve. Born: 15 March 1919, Charlotte, Mich. Accredited to: Michigan.

"Citation: For conspicuous devotion to duty and extraordinary courage and complete disregard of his own life, above and beyond the call of duty, during the attack on the Fleet at Pearl Harbor, by Japanese forces on 7 December 1941. When it was seen that the **USS OKLAHOMA** was going to capsize and the order was given to abandon ship, Ensign Flaherty remained in a turret, holding a flashlight so the remainder of the turret crew could see to escape, thereby sacrificing his own life."

* Posthumous award

•LIEUTENANT COMMANDER SAMUEL GLENN FUQUA, USN

"Rank and organization: Captain, U.S. Navy, **USS ARIZONA.** Place and date: Pearl Harbor, Territory of Hawaii, 7 December 1941. Entered service at: Laddonia, Mo. Born: 15 October 1899, Laddonia, Mo.

"Citation: For distinguished conduct in action, outstanding heroism, and utter disregard of his own safety above and beyond the call of duty during the attack on the Fleet in Pearl Harbor, by Japanese forces on 7 December 1941. Upon the commencement of the attack, Lieutenant Commander Fuqua rushed to the quarterdeck of the **USS ARIZONA** to which he was attached, where he was stunned and knocked down by the explosion of a large bomb which hit the quarterdeck, penetrated several decks, and started a severe fire. Upon regaining consciousness, he began to direct the fighting of the fire and the rescue of wounded and injured personnel. Almost immediately there was a tremendous explosion forward, which made the ship appear to rise out of the water, shudder, and settle down by the bow rapidly. The whole forward part of the ship was enveloped in flames which spread rapidly, and wounded and burned men poured out of the ship to the quarterdeck. Despite these conditions, his harrowing experience, and severe enemy bombing and strafing at the time, LCDR Fuqua continued to direct fighting of fires in order to check them while wounded and burned could be taken from the ship and supervised the rescue of these men in such an amazingly calm and cool manner and with such excellent judgment that it inspired everyone who saw him and undoubtedly resulted in saving of many lives. After realizing the ship could not be saved and that he was the senior surviving officer aboard, he directed it to be abandoned, but continued to remain on the quarterdeck and directed abandoning ship and rescue of personnel until satisfied that all personnel that could be had been saved, after which he left his ship with the last boatload. The conduct of LCDR Fuqua was not only in keeping with the highest traditions of the naval service but characterizes him as an outstanding leader of men."

• Deceased as of January 1987

*CHIEF BOATSWAIN EDWIN JOSEPH HILL, USN

"Rank and organization: Chief Boatswain, U.S. Navy. Born: 4 October 1894, Philadelphia, Pa. Accredited to: Pennsylvania.

"Citation: For distinguished conduct in the line of his profession, extraordinary courage, and disregard of his own safety during the attack on the Fleet in Pearl Harbor, by Japanese forces on 7 December 1941. During the height of the strafing and bombing, Chief Boatswain Hill led his men of the line-handling details of the **USS NEVADA** to the quays, cast off the lines and swam back to his ship. Later, while on the forecastle, attempting to let go the anchors, he was blown overboard and killed by the explosion of several bombs."

* Posthumous award

*ENSIGN HERBERT CHARPIOT JONES, USNR

"Rank and organization: Ensign, U.S. Naval Reserve. Born: 1 December 1918, Los Angeles, Calif. Accredited to: California.

"Citation: For conspicuous devotion to duty, extraordinary courage, and complete disregard of his own life, above and beyond the call of duty, during the attack on the Fleet in Pearl Harbor, by Japanese forces on 7 December 1941, Ens. Jones organized and led a party, which was supplying ammunition to the antiaircraft battery of the **USS CALIFORNIA** after the mechanical hoists were put out of action when he was fatally wounded by a bomb explosion. When 2 men attempted to take him from the area which was on fire, he refused to let them do so, saying in words to the effect, 'Leave me alone! I am done for. Get out of here before the magazines go off.' "

*Posthumous award

*REAR ADMIRAL ISAAC C. KIDD, USN

"Rank and organization Rear Admiral, U.S. Navy. Born: 26 March 1884, Cleveland, Ohio. Appointed from: Ohio.

"Citation: For conspicuous devotion to duty, extraordinary courage and complete disregard of his own life, during the attack on the Fleet in Pearl Harbor, by Japanese forces on 7 December 1941, Rear Adm. Kidd immediately went to the bridge and, as Commander Battleship Division One, courageously discharged his duties as Senior Officer Present Afloat until the **USS ARIZONA,** his Flagship, blew up from magazine explosions and a direct bomb hit on the bridge which resulted in the loss of his life."
*Posthumous award

•GUNNER JACKSON CHARLES PHARRIS, USN

"Rank and organization: Lieutenant, U.S. Navy, **USS CALIFORNIA**. Place and date: Pearl Harbor, Territory of Hawaii, 7 December 1941. Entered service at: California. Born: 26 June 1912, Columbus, Ga.

"Citation: For conspicuous gallantry and intrepidity at the risk of his life above and beyond the call of duty while attached to the **USS CALIFORNIA** during the surprise enemy Japanese aerial attack on Pearl Harbor, Territory of Hawaii, 7 December 1941. In charge of the ordnance repair party on the third deck when the first Japanese torpedo struck almost directly under his station, Lt. (then Gunner) Pharris was stunned and severely injured by the concussion which hurled him to the overhead and back to the deck. Quickly recovering, he acted on his own initiative to set up a hand-supply ammunition train for the anti-aircraft guns. With water and oil rushing in where the port bulkhead had been torn up from the deck, with many of the remaining crewmembers (sic) overcome by oil fumes, and the ship without power and listing heavily to port as a result of a second torpedo hit, Lt. Pharris ordered the shipfitters to counterflood. Twice rendered unconscious by the nauseous fumes and handicapped by his painful injuries, he persisted in his desperate efforts to speed up the supply of

ammunition and at the same time repeatedly risked his life to enter flooding compartments and drag to safety unconscious shipmates who were gradually being submerged in oil. By his inspiring leadership, his valiant efforts and his extreme loyalty to his ship and her crew, he saved many of his shipmates from death and was largely responsible for keeping the **CALIFORNIA** in action during the attack. His heroic conduct throughout this first eventful engagement of World War II reflects the highest credit upon Lt. Pharris and enhances the finest traditions of the U.S. Naval Service."
NOTE: Pharris received his Medal which was up-graded from a Navy Cross at the White House from President Truman 25 June 1948. Because of this discrepancy he is not listed with the original fourteen recipients.

•Deceased as of 1965

*CHIEF RADIOMAN THOMAS J. REEVES, USN

"Rank and organization: Radio Electrician (Warrant Officer) U.S. Navy. Born: 9 December 1895, Thomaston, Conn. Accredited to: Connecticut.

"Citation: For distinguished conduct in the line of his profession, extraordinary courage and disregard of his own safety during the attack on the Fleet in Pearl Harbor, by Japanese forces on 7 December 1941. After the mechanized ammunition hoists were put out of action in the **USS CALIFORNIA,** Reeves, on his own initiative, in a burning passageway, assisted in the maintenance of an ammunition supply by hand to the antiaircraft guns until he was overcome by smoke and fire, which resulted in his death."

*Posthumous award

MACHINIST DONALD K. ROSS, USN

"Rank and organization: Machinist, U.S. Navy, **USS NEVADA**. Place and date: Pearl Harbor, Territory of Hawaii, 7 December 1941. Entered service at: Denver, Colo. Born: 8 December 1910, Beverly, Kans.

"Citation: For distinguished conduct in the line of his profession, extraordinary courage and disregard of his own life during the attack on the Fleet in Pearl Harbor, Territory of Hawaii, by Japanese forces on 7 December 1941. When his station in the forward dynamo room of the **USS NEVADA** became almost untenable due to smoke, steam and heat, Machinist Ross forced his men to leave that station and performed all the duties himself until blinded and unconscious. Upon being rescued and resuscitated, he returned and secured the forward dynamo room and proceeded to the after dynamo room where he was later again rendered unconscious by exhaustion. Again recovering consciousness he returned to his station where he remained until directed to abandon it."

*MACHINIST MATE ROBERT R. SCOTT, USN

"Rank and organization: Machinist's Mate First Class, U.S. Navy. Born: 13 July 1915, Massillon, Ohio. Accredited to: Ohio.

"Citation: For conspicuous devotion to duty, extraordinary courage and complete disregard of his own life, above and beyond the call of duty, during the attack on the Fleet in Pearl Harbor by Japanese forces on 7 December 1941. The compartment, in the **USS CALIFORNIA,** in which the air compressor, to which Scott was assigned as his battle station, was flooded as a result of a torpedo hit. The remainder of the personnel evacuated that compartment but Scott refused to leave, saying words to the effect: "This is my station and I will stay and give them air as long as the guns are going."

*Posthumous award

*CHIEF WATERTENDER PETER TOMICH, USN

"Rank and organization: Chief Watertender, U.S. Navy. Born: 3 June 1893, Prolog, Austria, Accredited to: New Jersey.

"Citation: For distinguished conduct in the line of his profession, and extraordinary courage and disregard of his own safety, during the attack on the Fleet in Pearl Harbor by the Japanese forces on 7 December 1941. Although realizing that the ship was capsizing, as a result of enemy bombing and torpedoing, Tomich remained at his post in the engineering plant of the **USS UTAH,** until he saw that all boilers were secured and all fireroom personnel had left their stations, and by so doing lost his own life."
*Posthumous award

*CAPTAIN FRANKLIN VAN VALKENBURGH, USN

"Rank and organization: Captain, U.S. Navy. Born: 5 April 1888, Minneapolis, Minn. Appointed from: Wisconsin.

"Citation: For conspicuous devotion to duty, extraordinary courage and complete disregard of his own life, during the attack on the Fleet in Pearl Harbor, T. H. by Japanese forces on 7 December 1941. As commanding officer of the **USS ARIZONA,** Capt. Van Valkenburgh gallantly fought his ship until the **USS ARIZONA** blew up from magazine explosions and a direct bomb hit on the bridge which resulted in the loss of his life."
*Posthumous award

*SEAMAN FIRST CLASS JAMES R. WARD, USN

"Rank and organization: Seaman First Class, U.S. Navy. Born: 10 September 1921, Springfield, Ohio. Entered service at: Springfield, Ohio.

"Citation: For conspicuous devotion to duty, extraordinary courage and complete disregard of his life, above and beyond the call of duty, during the attack on the Fleet in Pearl Harbor by Japanese forces on 7 December 1941. When it was seen that the **USS OKLAHOMA** was going to capsize and the order was given to abandon ship, Ward remained in a turret holding a flashlight so the remainder of the turret crew could see to escape, thereby sacrificing his own life."

*Posthumous award

•COMMANDER CASSIN YOUNG, USN

"Rank and organization: Commander, U.S. Navy. Born: 6 March 1894, Washington, D.C. Appointed from: Wisconsin. Other Navy award: Navy Cross.

"Citation: For distinguished conduct in action, outstanding heroism and utter disregard of his own safety, above and beyond the call of duty, as commanding officer of the **USS VESTAL,** during the attack on the Fleet in Pearl Harbor, Territory of Hawaii, by enemy Japanese forces on 7 December 1941, Cmdr. Young proceeded to the bridge and later took personal command of the 3-inch antiaircraft gun. When blown overboard by the blast of the forward magazine explosion of the **USS ARIZONA,** to which the **USS VESTAL** was moored, he swam back to his ship. The entire forward part of the **USS ARIZONA** was a blazing inferno with oil afire on the water between the 2 ships; as a result of several bomb hits, the **USS VESTAL** was afire in several places, was settling and taking on a list. Despite severe enemy bombing and strafing at the time, and his shocking experience of having been blown overboard, Cmdr. Young, with extreme coolness and calmness, moved his ship to an anchorage distant from the **USS ARIZONA,** and subsequently beached the **USS VESTAL** upon determining that such action was required to save his ship."
•Captain Young was killed November 1942 during the battle of Savo Island near Guadalcanal.
* Posthumous award

Navy Cross

NAVY CROSS

CRITERIA FOR NAVY CROSS

The Navy Cross is awarded to any person serving with the Naval Service who distinguishes himself by extraordinary heroism in connection with military operations against an armed enemy, such heroism not being sufficient to justify the award of the Medal of Honor.

DESCRIPTION

The medal is made of bronze and consists of a maltese cross with leaves of a wreath protruding between the arms of the cross; on the obverse the cross is surmounted by a button in the center containing a caravel of the time of Columbus.

On the reverse of the cross there is a button containing two crossed anchors with the letters U.S.N. The medal is suspended from a ribbon of dark blue with a white stripe in the center.[1]

NAVY CROSS

LIEUTENANT COMMANDER LAURENCE (sic) A. ABERCROM-
  BIE, U.S. NAVY
LIEUTENANT COMMANDER WILLIAM L. ANDERSON, U.S.
  NAVY
CHIEF CARPENTER JOHN ARNOLD AUSTIN, U.S. NAVY
PHARMACIST MATE SECOND CLASS LIONEL H. BAKER, U.S.
  NAVY
LIEUTENANT (jg) GORDON E. BOLSER, U.S. NAVY
BOATSWAIN ADOLPH MARCUS BOTHNE, U.S. NAVY
LIEUTENANT COMMANDER WILLIAM P. BURFORD, U.S. NAVY
LIEUTENANT HIRAM CASSEDY, U.S. NAVY
*ENSIGN HARALD (sic) J. CHRISTOPHER, U.S. NAVAL RESERVE
ENSIGN GEORGE COOK, U.S. NAVY
COMMANDER WINFIELD S. CUNNINGHAM, U.S. NAVY

1. Bunkley, Capt. J.W., USN, MILITARY AND NAVAL RECOGNITION BOOK, D. Van
   Nostrand Company, Inc. NY NY, 1941

PHARMACIST MATE SECOND CLASS NED B. CURTIS, U.S. NAVY
*COXSWAIN EDWARD CARLYLE DALY, U.S. NAVY
PRIVATE FIRST CLASS WILLIARD D. DARLING, U.S. MARINE
  CORPS
*ENSIGN FREDERICK C. DAVIS, U.S. NAVAL RESERVE
LIEUTENANT COMMANDER JOHN L. DETAR, U.S. NAVY
MAJOR JAMES P.S. DEVEREAUX, U.S. MARINE CORPS
LIEUTENANT CLARENCE E. DICKENSON, Jr., U.S. NAVY
SECOND LIEUTENANT ROBERT L. DICKEY, U.S. NAVY
AVIATION CHIEF MACHINIST MATE HAROLD E. DIXON, U.S.
  NAVY
GUNNERY SERGEANT CHARLES S. DOUGLASS, U.S. MARINE
  CORPS
CORPORAL JOSEPH RICHARD DRISKELL, U.S. MARINE CORPS
ENSIGN ERNEST H. DUNLAP, U.S. NAVY
LIEUTENANT JOHN M. EATON, Jr., U.S. NAVAL RESERVE
ENSIGN JOHN PERRY EDWARDS, U.S. NAVAL RESERVE
ENSIGN JOSEPH EKAR, U.S. NAVY
CHIEF SHIPFITTER GEORGE DANIEL ETCELL, U.S. NAVY
LIEUTENANT FRANK W. FENNO, U.S. NAVY
*ENSIGN FRANK MOORE FISLER, U.S. NAVAL RESERVE
BOATSWAINS MATE FIRST CLASS, WILLIAM S. FLEMING, U.S.
  NAVY
ENSIGN C.F. GIMBER, U.S. NAVAL RESERVE
SEAMAN SECOND CLASS LOUIS G. GOMBASY, U.S. NAVY
AVIATION MACHINIST MATE FIRST CLASS DONALD A.
  GRAHAM, U.S. NAVY
LIEUTENANT COMMANDER ELTON E. GRENFELL, U.S. NAVY
SERGEANT THOMAS E. HAILEY, U.S. MARINE CORPS
CHIEF MACHINIST MATE ALFRED LAWRENCE HANSEN, U.S.
  NAVY
CORPORAL HAROLD R. HAZELWOOD, U.S. MARINE CORPS
COMMANDER WILLIAM R. HOLLINGSWORTH, U.S. NAVY
ENSIGN ALLEN J. HUTTENBERG, U.S. NAVAL RESERVE
LIEUTENANT COMMANDER SOLOMON C. ISQUITH, U.S. NAVY
COMMANDER JESSE D. JEWELL, MEDICAL CORPS, U.S. NAVY
*LIEUTENANT DRAPER KAUFFMAN, U.S. NAVAL RESERVE
ENSIGN NILS R. LARSON, U.S. NAVY
LIEUTENANT COMMANDER WILLIS A. LENT, U.S. NAVY

FIREMAN SECOND CLASS F.C. LEY, Jr., U.S. NAVAL RESERVE
AVIATION CHIEF MACHINIST MATE JOHN T. MARQUIS, U.S. NAVY
CAPTAIN FRANCIS P. McCARTHY, U.S. MARINE CORPS
BOATSWAINS MATE FIRST CLASS PAUL JAMES McMURTRY, U.S. NAVY
RADIOMAN SECOND CLASS HARRY R. MEAD, U.S. NAVY
MESS ATTENDANT SECOND CLASS DORIS MILLER, U.S. NAVY
ENSIGN JIM DICK MILLER, U.S. NAVY
*SEAMAN FIRST CLASS FRED KENNETH MOORE, U.S. NAVY
*LIEUTENANT COMMANDER STANLEY P. MOSELEY, U.S. NAVY
ENSIGN GEORGE D. MURRAY, U.S. NAVY
CAPTAIN JAMES L. NEEFUS, U.S. NAVY
LIEUTENANT WILLIAM W. OUTERBRIDGE, U.S. NAVY
SEAMAN FIRST CLASS WILLIAM WHITEFORD PARKER, U.S. NAVY
LIEUTENANT COMMANDER LEWIS S. PARKS, U.S. NAVY
CORPORAL DALE L. PETERS, U.S. MARINE CORPS
RADIOMAN SECOND CLASS ROBERT J. PETERSON, U.S. NAVY
#GUNNER JACKSON C. PHARRIS, U.S. NAVY
COMMANDER JOHN S. PHILLIPS, U.S. NAVY
LIEUTENANT CECIL D. RIGGS, MEDICAL CORPS, U.S. NAVY
LIEUTENANT (jg) JAMES W. ROBB, Jr., U.S. NAVY
RADIOMAN SECOND CLASS WILLIAM R. ROBERTS, U.S. NAVY
ENSIGN WESLEY H. RUTH, U.S. NAVY
ENSIGN ARNOLD D. SINGLETON, U.S. NAVAL RESERVE
LIEUTENANT COMMANDER CHESTER C. SMITH, U.S. NAVY
BOATSWAINS MATE SECOND CLASS HAROLD FRANCIS SMITH, U.S. NAVY
YEOMAN FIRST CLASS JAMES L. SNYDER, U.S. NAVY
*FIRST LIEUTENANT CHARLES W. SOMERS, Jr., U.S. MARINE CORPS
ENSIGN JOSEPH K. TAUSSIG, Jr., U.S. NAVY
ENSIGN THOMAS H. TAYLOR, U.S. NAVY
ENSIGN PERRY L. TEAFF, U.S. NAVY
AVIATION MACHINIST MATE SECOND CLASS ALBERT CURTIS THATCHER, U.S. NAVY
LIEUTENANT COMMANDER FRANCIS J. THOMAS, U.S. NAVAL RESERVE
ENSIGN ROBERT E. THOMAS, Jr., U.S. NAVY

FIREMAN SECOND CLASS JOHN BARTH VAESSEN, U.S. NAVAL RESERVE
LIEUTENANT COMMANDER WILLIAM F. VERDEN, U.S. NAVY
AVIATION MACHINIST MATE L.H. WAGONER, U.S. NAVY
LIEUTENANT COMMANDER FREDERICK B. WARDER, U.S. NAVY
LIEUTENANT COMMANDER DAVID C. WHITE , U.S. NAVY
LIEUTENANT COMMANDER CHARLES W. WILKENS, U.S. NAVY

* Posthumous award
\# Graded up to Medal of Honor several years later

NAVY CROSS CITATIONS

LIEUTENANT COMMANDER LAURENCE A. ABERCROMBIE, U.S. NAVY

"For distinguished service in line of his profession as Commanding Officer of **USS DRAYTON** on December 24, 1941 conducting operations with that destroyer which resulted in the destruction of an enemy vessel."

LIEUTENANT COMMANDER WILLIAM L. ANDERSON, U.S. NAVY

"For his participation February 1, 1942 in the attack on the Marshall Islands."

*CHIEF CARPENTER JOHN ARNOLD AUSTIN, U.S. NAVY

"For exceptional courage, presence of mind, and devotion to duty during the Japanese attack on the United States Pacific Fleet in Pearl Harbor, Territory of Hawaii on December 7, 1941. When the **USS OKLAHOMA** capsized, he and a number of the crew were entrapped in one of the ship's compartments. By his efforts, a porthole which was under water was located and he assisted fifteen of the crew to escape. He gallantly gave up his life in the service of his country. His conduct was in keeping with the highest traditions of the naval service."

PHARMACIST MATE SECOND CLASS LIONEL H. BAKER, U.S. NAVY

"For distinguished service in line of his profession when, on the repair ship **USS VESTAL,** to which he was attached, he cared for the wounded in an outstanding manner, although suffering from shrapnel wounds himself."

LIEUTENANT (jg) GORDON E. BOLSER, U.S. NAVY

"For distinguished service in line of his profession, extraordinary courage and disregard of his own safety, during the attack on the Fleet in Pearl Harbor, Territory of Hawaii, by Japanese forces on December 7, 1941. Although contact with the enemy meant almost certain destruction and despite the lack of any armament in this type plane, Lieutenant Bolser voluntarily piloted a JRS amphibian plane, equipped only with Springfield rifles in search for and to obtain information of the enemy forces."

BOATSWAIN ADOLPH MARCUS BOTHNE, U.S. NAVY

"For distinguished devotion to duty, extraordinary courage, and utter disregard of his own safety during the attack on the Fleet in Pearl Harbor, Territory of Hawaii, by Japanese forces on December 7, 1941. Upon the **USS OKLAHOMA** capsizing within ten minutes after the attack began, Boatswain Bothne pulled himself into a motor launch of which he acted as coxswain. By skillful handling, he succeeded in picking up a boatload of survivors from the water and landed them at Ford Island. He then returned to the vicinity of the **USS OKLAHOMA** and rescued another boatload of survivors, all who remained in sight of that area, and landed them at Ford Island also. Thereafter throughout the remainder of the attack, despite severe bombing and strafing, he patrolled the battleship line in search of more survivors. Furthermore, subsequent to the attack, he assisted most efficiently in fighting fires and in the rescue of personnel trapped in the **USS OKLAHOMA.**"
NOTE: See the section, NAVY AND MARINE COPRS MEDALS, for Bothne's additional award for action of February 7, 1942.

LIEUTENANT COMMANDER WILLIAM P. BURFORD, U.S. NAVY

"For distinguished service in line of his profession as Commanding Officer, **USS MONAGHAN,** during the attack on the Fleet in Pearl Harbor, Territory of Hawaii, by Japanese forces on December 7, 1941. During the sortie of the **USS MONAGHAN,** from Pearl Harbor, a Japanese submarine was sighted in the harbor. Despite the severe enemy bombing and strafing at the time, LCDR Burford, through skillful handling of his ship at high speed in the shoal water and at a bend in the channel, attacked and destroyed the submarine by ramming and with depth charges; and completed the sortie from the harbor in an outstanding manner."

LIEUTENANT HIRAM CASSEDY, U.S. NAVY

For a submarine rescue of an Australian aviator stranded on the Island of Timor when the Japanese invaded the southwest Pacific Islands in the Spring of 1942. "While C.O. of the **USS SEARAVEN** on April 18-19, 1942, you were directed to evacuate a number of airmen of the Royal Australian Air Force from Timor, N.E.I. The island was occupied by the enemy. Enemy forces were aware of the presence of the party of distressed aviators and operations were in progress to capture the group. You safely conducted your vessel to the rendezvous under hazardous conditions of navigation and by virtue of thorough preparations and excellent foresight effected a contact with the Australians. Although the area was under constant enemy patrol your vessel remained undetected. Under trying conditions and with the utmost pertinacity you directed the recovery of the aviators who were in an emaciated and fever ridden state.

"The exceptional heroism displayed by you and the officers and men of the **USS SEARAVEN** is a tribute to your leadership and skill and is in accord with the best traditions of the Navy of the United States."

*ENSIGN HARALD J. CHRISTOPHER, U.S. NAVAL RESERVE

"For distinguished service, extraordinary courage and devotion to duty and disregard of his own safety during the attack on the Fleet in Pearl Harbor, T.H. by Japanese forces on December 7, 1941. Ensign Christopher, realizing his services at this regular battle station on the **USS NEVADA** were not needed at the time, he, on his own initiative, assumed duties on the five-inch broadside battery and effectively controlled his part of that battery until killed by a bomb explosion."

ENSIGN GEORGE COOK, U.S. NAVY

"On the night of April 18 and 19, 1942, you were in charge of the boat and rescue party seeking to evacuate a group of distressed Australian aviators, grounded on the island of Timor, N.E.I. Enemy forces were present in the vicinity and searching for the party. You swam ashore through the surf and after considerable difficulty and with great danger to yourself, made contact with the Australians. You made several trips through the surf, superintended the transfer of the sick and wounded men to the **USS SEAHAVEN** and saved two from drowning. You displayed extraordinary heroism under exceptionally trying conditions.

"Your actions were in complete disregard of your personal safety and are an inspiring example of devotion to duty. Your high courage and fine leadership on this occasion are in accord with the best traditions of the Navy of the United States."

COMMANDER WINFIELD S. CUNNINGHAM, U.S. NAVY

"For distinguished and heroic conduct in the line of his profession, as commanding officer, naval air station, Wake Island, where he was responsible for directing defenses of that post during the Japanese seige from December 7-22, 1941, against impossible odds."

NOTE: Commander Cunningham was taken prisoner by the Japanese when they captured Wake. He remained a POW until war's end.

PHARMACIST MATE SECOND CLASS NED B. CURTIS, U.S. NAVY

"For outstanding courage during the attack by Japanese forces on the Fleet at Pearl Harbor, December 7, 1941. Acting on orders to evacuate the control officers starboard antiaircraft battery of a battleship **(NEVADA),** he climbed the foremast to the director under heavy enemy bombing and strafing which were causing heavy casualties. He disregarded orders of the wounded officer, Ensign Joseph K. Taussig, Jr., to go below. Placing him in a stretcher, and with the assistance of other men, he lowered him three deck levels to the boat deck when other means of descent were blocked by a serious fire caused by a bomb hit. He was burned so severely as to cause his subsequent removal to a hospital."

NOTE: Curtis retired from the Navy as a Captain in the Medical Service Corps.

*COXSWAIN EDWARD CARLYLE DALY, U.S. NAVY

"For distinguished service and devotion to duty when, on December 7, 1941, after an oil fire forced the abandonment of his station in the forward part of his ship, the **USS DOWNES,** a destroyer which was heavily bombed during the attack, he gave up his life in a courageous and daring attempt to save a badly wounded shipmate who had been trapped in a flaming compartment of the ship."

PRIVATE FIRST CLASS WILLIARD D. DARLING, U.S. MARINE CORPS

"For outstanding courage during the Japanese attack on the Fleet at Pearl Harbor, December 7, 1941. "As he was being evacuated from the **USS OKLAHOMA** in a motor launch, he saw an officer apparently drowning in the water. He dove from the boat, swam to the officer, and kept him afloat until rescued by a second launch. Subsequently, he brought the exhausted officer ashore after both had been forced to abandon this craft. Throughout the entire period, they were under heavy enemy bombing and strafing."

*ENSIGN FREDERICK C. DAVIS, U.S. NAVAL RESERVE

"For initiative and disregard of his own safety during the Japanese attack on the Fleet at Pearl Harbor, December 7, 1941. Since no planes were on board his battleship, **USS NEVADA,** this aviator on his own initiative and in a heroic effort to be of the greatest usefulness, was hurrying to the foremast structure to take charge of the forward antiaircraft machine gun battery when he was killed by a bomb explosion."

LIEUTENANT COMMANDER JOHN L. DETAR, U.S. NAVY

"For bravery and determination when he led his ship against the enemy in the enemy's own waters. In the face of strong Japanese surface patrols he sank much enemy shipping and damaged others. His vessel returned without material or personal losses."

MAJOR JAMES P.S. DEVEREAUX, U.S. MARINE CORPS

"For distinguished and heroic conduct in the line of his profession, as Commanding Officer of the Marine defense battalion, Naval Air Station, Wake Island, where he was responsible for directing defenses of that post during the Japenese siege from December 7-22, 1941, against impossible odds."

LIEUTENANT CLARENCE E. DICKENSON, Jr., U.S. NAVY

"This officer, a **USS ENTERPRISE** pilot was awarded the NAVY CROSS with gold star* for his actions on December 7 and 10, 1941. Returning to Oahu in a scouting plane, he and his gunner were engaged by a superior number of Japanese aircraft. Although the latter was killed, Lt. Dickinson continued to engage the enemy until his plane was forced down

in flames. He escaped by parachute, landed near Ewa field, and proceeded to the naval air station, Ford Island, Pearl Harbor. Here he was immediately assigned to a 175 mile aerial search operation at sea, his recent ordeal not having been reported. On December 10 he attacked and possibly destroyed an enemy submarine.
*In lieu of a second Navy Cross for a separate action."

LIEUTENANT ROBERT L. DICKEY, U.S. MARINE CORPS

"For action during Japanese attacks on Midway Island, December 7, 1941 to May 7, 1942. Lieutenant Robert L. Dickey, then Marine Gunner, exhibited heroism and tenacity in pressing the aerial attack and skillful maneuvering of aircraft in attacks on enemy aircraft."

AVIATION CHIEF MACHINIST MATE HAROLD DIXON, U.S. NAVY

"For extraordinary heroism, exceptional determination and skillful seamanship when, after a forced landing at sea against the enemy January 18, 1942, his plane sank immediately forcing him and his crew to take to an aviation emergency rubber boat. By his resourcefulness and excellent judgment he succeeded in navigating the rubber boat for 34 days over approximately 500 miles, without adequate provisions or equipment, and landing safely on a remote Pacific Island, thereby saving the lives of his crew and exhibiting the highest quality of leadership."

GUNNERY SERGEANT CHARLES S. DOUGLASS, U.S. MARINE CORPS

"For exceptionally meritorious service and extraordinary courage during the Japanese attack on the Fleet at Pearl Harbor, December 7, 1941. On board the battleship **USS NEVADA,** in charge of forward antiaircraft machine guns which kept continuous action until two circulating lines were hit, burst and unable to cool the weapons, he remained at his station with his men, firing the remaining guns until the end of the action in the face of a dangerous conflagration."

CORPORAL JOSEPH RICHARD DRISKELL, U.S. MARINE CORPS

"For initiative and disregard of his own safety, during the Japanese attack on the Fleet at Pearl Harbor, December 7, 1941. As #7 broadside gun captain on the battleship **USS NEVADA,** although wounded and with most of his clothes burned off, he manned another gun when his own was wrecked. Subsequently he assisted other injured men and joined in fire-fighting squads which brought flames under control."

ENSIGN ERNEST H. DUNLAP, Jr., U.S. NAVY

"For distinguished service in line of his profession, exceptional courage, coolness and devotion to duty during the attack on the Fleet in Pearl Harbor, Territory of Hawaii, by Japanese forces on December 7, 1941. When Ensign Dunlap found that his services in the foretop as Spotter on the **USS NEVADA** were not required, he joined the secondary battery, supervised the manning of guns and organization of ammunition supply, and maintained an accurate fire on low flying enemy aircraft until seriously wounded by the explosion of an enemy bomb. Despite his wounded condition, he assisted with the wounded until he himself collapsed."

LIEUTENANT JOHN M. EATON, Jr., U.S. NAVAL RESERVE

"For extraordinary heroism while serving as a ground officer of Patrol Squadron 21 temporarily based at the Naval Air Station, Midway Island, during the attack by Japanese naval forces on the night of December 7, 1941. When devastating hostile gunfire damaged or destroyed several Catalina flying boats, the hangar and other installations, Ensign Eaton organized a crew of untrained civilian workmen and, without benefit of tractors and lines, ingeniously directed the launching of heavily overloaded aircraft. In the cold water of the lagoon and on a ramp which was flooded with gasoline from damaged airplanes and lighted by a conflagration nearby, he valiantly and resolutely continued his work without regard for his safety until all Catalinas capable of flight had been launched. Although completely unfamiliar with aviation, Ensign Eaton, by his courageous initiative and tenacious determination, successfully executed this highly technical operation and thereby undoubtedly contributed to the Japanese abandonment of their attack, consequently saving the islands from more extensive damage."

ENSIGN JOHN PERRY EDWARDS, U.S. NAVAL RESERVE

"For distinguished service in line of his profession, extraordinary courage and disregard of his own safety during the attack on the Fleet in Pearl Harbor, Territory of Hawaii, by Japanese forces on December 7, 1941. Although contact with the enemy meant almost certain destruction and despite the lack of any armament in this type plane, Ensign Edwards voluntarily piloted a JRS amphibian plane, equipped only with Springfield rifles, in search for and to obtain information of the enemy forces."

ENSIGN JOSEPH EKAR, U.S. NAVY

"For extraordinary heroism on January 10, 1942, as commander of the ready duty patrol plane, Fleet Air Detachment, San Diego, California. You accomplished the successful rescue at sea of Captain Graham E. Benson, USMC, and Corporal C.S. Pierson, USMC, who, after a forced landing of their plane, were adrift at sea in a small aviation emergency rubber boat. When the rescue boat you directed to their aid became disabled, you skillfully and courageously landed your plane in a very unfavorable sea and took off parallel to the swells without injury to any personnel or to your plane."

CHIEF SHIPFITTER GEORGE DANIEL ETCELL, U.S. NAVY

"For distinguished service in line of his profession, extraordinary courage and disregard of his own safety during the attack on the Fleet in Pearl Harbor, Territory of Hawaii, by Japanese forces on December 7, 1941. While handling fires, flooding and damage control, he was ordered to determine whether a forward magazine group on his battleship, **USS NEVADA,** had been flooded. He unhesitatingly risked his life passing through hot water more than waist deep and heavy smoke in order to obtain the information. In this area he came upon an unconscious shipmate whom he carried to safety."

LIEUTENANT COMMANDER FRANK W. FENNO, U.S. NAVY

"For exceptionally meritorious service in a duty of great responsibility, as Commanding Officer of the **USS TROUT,**[1] in successfully completing an unusual and special mission through enemy controlled waters for the United States War Department during the month of January 1942. Upon completion of this mission, and while returning to Pearl Harbor, Territory of Hawaii, through enemy infested waters, with a special cargo on board, the **USS TROUT** attacked and sank a 5000 ton enemy merchant vessel on February 10, 1942. Furthermore, on the same date, upon being attacked by torpedoes from an enemy patrol vessel, the **USS TROUT** attacked and sank the enemy attacking ship, and continued her voyage to Pearl Harbor, arriving there without damage to material or injury to personnel throughout the hazardous operations."

1. **TROUT** was responsible for bringing the gold out of the Philippines.

ENSIGN FRANK MOORE FISLER, U.S. NAVAL RESERVE

"For extraordinary courage and heroic conduct as first pilot of a navy seaplane, Ensign Fisler, against insurmountable odds, rescued nine army fliers (including an officer) of an Army plane that had been forced down far from Oahu during combat."

BOATSWAINS MATE FIRST CLASS WILLIAM S. FLEMING, U.S. NAVY

"For devotion to duty and extraordinary coolness while serving as gun captain on a battleship during the Japanese attack on the Fleet at Pearl Harbor, Territory of Hawaii, December 7, 1941. Although injured, he kept at his post as gun captain, directing his crew in such a cool and outstanding manner that it inspired confidence in the men about him."

ENSIGN C. F. GIMBER, U.S. NAVAL RESERVE

"As second pilot of a navy seaplane whose crew and officers, against insurmountable odds, rescued nine army flyers (including one officer) of an army plane that had been forced down to sea during combat far from Oahu."

SEAMAN SECOND CLASS LOUIS G. GOMBASY, U.S. NAVY

"For initiative and extraordinary courage during the Japanese attack on Pearl Harbor, Territory of Hawaii, December 7, 1941. When S2c Gombasy heard a bomb strike the deck of the battleship **USS NEVADA** on which he was stationed, he left his station in a turret to assist in clearing mooring lines that the vessel might get underway. Wounded, he continued to clear lines, help other injured personnel and fight fires."

AVIATION MACHINIST MATE FIRST CLASS DONALD A. GRAHAM, U.S. NAVY

"For initiative, extraordinary courage and coolness during the Japanese attack on Pearl Harbor, Territory of Hawaii, December 7, 1941. Although his shipmates were leaving the blazing **USS ARIZONA,** on his own initiative he faced the intense fire on the deck, severe bombing and withering machine gun fire of enemy strafing planes to release lines connecting the battleship with a repair vessel, **USS VESTAL,** thus aiding the latter in getting underway."

0755: The Heroes of Pearl Harbor

LIEUTENANT COMMANDER ELTON E. GRENFELL, U.S. NAVY

"For distinguished service while engaged in hazardous submarine patrol duties in own and enemy waters. Lieutenant Commander Grenfell commanded his crew and ship to successfully attack and destroy enemy ships."

SERGEANT THOMAS E. HAILEY, U.S. MARINE CORPS

"For initiative, extraordinary courage and disregard for his own safety during the Japanese attack on the Fleet at Pearl Harbor, Territory of Hawaii, December 7, 1941. Stationed on the **USS OKLAHOMA,** when that battleship capsized, he swam to an adjacent battleship to assist in the rescue of the latter's crew. Then, on his own initiative he manned an antiaircraft gun, despite enemy bombing and strafing and the fact that he had no previous experience in this type of weapon. Later, clad only in his underwear and armed with a rifle, he volunteered and went up in an airplane on a five-hour search mission."

COMMANDER WILLIAM R. HOLLINGSWORTH, U.S. NAVY

"For extreme heroism and courageous devotion to duty as Commanding Officer of Bombing Squadron Six, **USS ENTERPRISE,** in action against enemy Japanese forces in Kwajalein Atoll, Marshall Islands, February 1, 1942. After leading his squadron over the enemy concentration, Commander Hollingsworth dove his plane through withering anti-aircraft fire and scored a direct bomb hit on an enemy anti-aircraft cruiser. Later in that day, he again led his squadron in a vigorous and successful attack on an enemy air base at Taroa Island, Maloelap Atoll, and despite intense anti-aircraft opposition, destroyed four enemy two-engined bombers and three Japanese fighters being serviced on the air field. His fine spirit of determination and initiative in offensive action and his gallant disregard for his own personal safety were in keeping with the highest traditions of the United States Naval Service."

CHIEF MACHINIST MATE ALFRED LAWRENCE HANSEN, U.S. NAVY

"For devotion to duty with utter disregard for his own safety during the Japanese attack on Pearl Harbor, December 7, 1941. Wounded in the severe enemy bombing and strafing attack on the Naval Air Station, Ford Island, Pearl Harbor, CMM Hansen, though wounded, continued to assist Ensign D.A. Singleton, USNR, in securing fuel lines at the air station, thus helping free the tanker, **USS NEOSHO,** that was fueling the station."

CORPORAL HAROLD R. HAZELWOOD, U.S. MARINE CORPS

"For exceptionally meritorious service, extraordinary courage and disregard of his own condition during the bombardment of Sand Island, Midway Islands, by Japanese forces on December 7, 1941. Corporal Hazelwood, the switchboard operator at the Command Post, Battery "H" Sixth Defense Battalion, Fleet Marine Force, U.S. Marine Corps, was wounded by shell fragments of a projectile that burst in the Command Post. Despite a compound-fractured leg, he immediately set up his switchboard again and reestablished communication."

ENSIGN ALLEN J. HUTTENBERG, U.S. NAVAL RESERVE

"For distinguished service in line of his profession, exceptional courage, coolness and devotion to duty during the attack on the Fleet in Pearl Harbor, Territory of Hawaii, by Japanese forces on December 7, 1941. Despite heavy enemy bombing, strafing and torpedo attacks, Ensign Huttenberg, battery officer on the 5" anti-aircraft battery of the **USS NEVADA,** although seriously wounded and handicapped by heavy casualties to the personnel of the battery, maintained a highly effective fire from his battery."

LIEUTENANT COMMANDER SOLOMON C. ISQUITH, U.S. NAVY

"For distinguished service in line of his profession as Commanding Officer of the **USS UTAH** during the attack on the Fleet in Pearl Harbor, Territory of Hawaii, by Japanese forces on December 7, 1941. With extraordinary courage and disregard of his own safety, Lieutenant Commander Isquith directed the abandonment of the ship when it was capsizing rapidly, in such a cool and efficient manner that approximately ninety per cent of the crew were saved."

COMMANDER JESSE D. JEWELL, MEDICAL CORPS, U.S. NAVY

"For distinguished service in line of his profession, extraordinary courage and disregard of his own condition during the attack on the Fleet in Pearl Harbor, Territory of Hawaii, by Japanese forces on December 7, 1941. Although burned about the face and arms from fires nearby his station on board the **USS CALIFORNIA,** he continued at this post of duty and administered effective first aid."

LIEUTENANT DRAPER L. KAUFMAN, U.S. NAVAL RESERVE

"For extraordinary heroism and devotion to duty. After the surprise bombing of the United States forces at and near Pearl Harbor, Territory of Hawaii by enemy Japanese aerial units on December 7, 1941, he unloaded and examined a live 500 pound Japanese bomb lying on the grounds of Fort Schofield, Oahu, Territory of Hawaii. His courage, confidence and exceptional skill made possible the recovery of all parts of this Japanese bomb for study by the Bureau of Ordnance of the Navy Department."

ENSIGN NILS R. LARSON, U.S. NAVY

"For distinguished service in line of his profession, extraordinary courage and disregard of his own safety during the attack on the Fleet in Pearl Harbor, Territory of Hawaii, by Japanese forces on December 7, 1941. Although contact with the enemy meant almost certain destruction and despite the lack of any armament in this type plane, Ensign Larson voluntarily piloted a JRS amphibian plane, equipped only with Springfield rifles, in search for and to obtain information of the enemy forces."

LIEUTENANT COMMANDER WILLIS A. LENT, U.S. NAVY

"Commanding a fleet submarine, Lieutenant Commander Willis A. Lent took his ship on an aggressive patrol against the enemy in hazardous waters. Despite Japanese air search he sank thousands of tons of Japanese shipping, also returning to base without damage to his submarine or personnel."

FIREMAN SECOND CLASS F.C. LEY, Jr., U.S. NAVAL RESERVE

"For devotion to duty with utter disregard for his own safety when serving as a member of a boat crew of the naval hospital ship **USS SOLACE,** during the attack on the Fleet in Pearl Harbor, Territory of Hawaii, by Japanese forces on December 7, 1941. When his boat was sent alongside the blazing **USS ARIZONA,** Fireman Second Class Ley displayed unusual disregard of his own life in diving overboard into water on which there was a great amount of burning oil, to save an officer from drowning."

CHIEF AVIATION MACHINIST MATE JOHN T. MARQUIS, U.S. NAVY

"For extraordinary heroism while acting as second pilot of the ready duty patrol plane, Fleet Air Detachment, San Diego, Calif., Jan. 20, 1942. You and your patrol plane commander, Ensign Joseph A. Ekar, A-V(N) USNR, successfully rescued at sea Capt. Graham E. Benson, USMC, and Corporal C.S. Pierson, USMC, who, after a forced landing of their plane, were adrift at sea in a small aviation emergency rubber boat. When the rescue boat which went to their aid was disabled, you assisted Ens. Ekar in skillfully and courageously landing your plane in very unfavorable seas, and in taking off parallel to the swells without injury to any personnel of the plane."

*CAPTAIN FRANCIS P. McCARTHY, U.S. MARINE CORPS

"For extraordinary heroism in the line of his profession as section leader, during the battle of Midway Islands on June 4, 1942. While leading his section against Japanese bomber and fighter aircraft, vastly superior in numbers, Captain McCarthy fearlessly pressed home his attack thereby seriously disrupting the plans of the enemy, lessening the effectiveness of their attack and contributing greatly to their defeat. As a result of his heroic action, and because of the circumstances attendant to the Battle of Midway Island, there can be no doubt that Captain McCarthy gave his life in the service of his country. His conduct throughout was in keeping with the highest traditions of the naval service."

BOATSWAIN'S MATE FIRST CLASS PAUL JAMES McMURTRY, U.S. NAVY

"For devotion to duty and exceptional courage, initiative and devotion to duty when serving on the **USS NEVADA** during the attack on the Fleet in Pearl Harbor, Territory of Hawaii, by Japanese forces on December, 1941. Realizing that main turrets of his ship would not be firing, he left his battle station and under heavy enemy strafing, bombing and torpedo attacks, formed relief gun crews to replace many casualties on antiaircraft batteries."

RADIOMAN SECOND CLASS HARRY R. MEAD, U.S. NAVY

"For devotion to duty and exceptional courage during the attack on the Fleet in Pearl Harbor, Territory of Hawaii, by Japanese forces on December 7, 1941. Although it was expected that his post in the Naval Air Station, Ford Island, Pearl Harbor, would be a major enemy target, and all other personnel were ordered to shelter, Radioman Second Class Mead stayed at his post throughout the attack. Later in the day, he volunteered as radioman-gunner in a plane assigned to a search mission."

MESS ATTENDANT SECOND CLASS DORIS MILLER, U.S. NAVY

"For devotion to duty, extraordinary courage and disregard for his own personal safety during the attack on Pearl Harbor by the Japanese,

December 7, 1941. While at the side of his Captain on the bridge of the battleship **USS WEST VIRGINIA,** Mess Attendant Second Class Doris Miller, despite enemy bombing and strafing, and in the face of serious fire, assisted in moving his Captain who had been mortally wounded, to a place of greater safety, and later manned and operated a machine-gun until ordered to leave the bridge."

NOTE: Miller, a sharecropper's son of Waco, Texas, was the first Negro (black) to merit the Navy Cross.

ENSIGN JIM DICK MILLER, U.S. NAVY

"For distinguished service in the line of his profession, extraordinary courage and disregard of his own safety during the attack on the Fleet in Pearl Harbor, Territory of Hawaii, by Japanese forces on December 7, 1941. Upon Turret III of the **USS ARIZONA** becoming untenable due to gas from a bomb hit on the quarterdeck penetrating several decks and starting a fire, Ensign Miller ordered his turret crew out to fight fires. Almost immediately, a tremendous explosion forward made the ship appear to rise our of the water, shudder and settle rapidly down by the bow. The whole forward part of the ship was enveloped in flames spreading rapidly; wounded and burned men poured onto the quarterdeck. Despite these conditions plus severe enemy bombing and strafing, Miller assisted in directing firefighting to check them while wounded and burned could be taken from the ship. He supervised their rescue in such an amazingly calm, cool manner and with such excellent judgment, it inspired everyone who saw him and undoubtedly resulted in saving many lives. After the abandon ship order he remained on the quarterdeck assisting in directing abandon ship and rescue of personnel, until satisfied that all personnel who could be, had been saved, after which he left his ship with the last boatload. Furthermore, after leaving his ship, on his own initiative he engineered a motor launch that proceeded to the quays and picked up personnel seeking protection there from the severe fires, and rescued many men from the water. The conduct of Ensign Miller on this occasion was in keeping with the highest traditions of the Naval Service."

*SEAMAN FIRST CLASS FRED KENNETH MOORE, U.S. NAVY

"For devotion to duty, extraordinary courage and disregard of his own safety during the attack on the Fleet in Pearl harbor, Territory of Hawaii, by Japanese forces, December 7, 1941. Despite orders from his gun captain to take cover, Seaman First Class Fred Kenneth Moore remained at his undermanned station with two other members of his antiaircraft gun crew under heavy enemy strafing. He assisted in keeping the gun in operation until he was killed at his station by an explosion."

LIEUTENANT COMMANDER STANLEY P. MOSELEY, U.S. NAVY

"For distinguished service while engaged in hazardous submarine patrol duties in own and enemy waters. Lieutenant Commander Stanley P. Moseley commanded his crew and ship to successfully attack and destroy many enemy ships.

CAPTAIN GEORGE D. MURRAY, U.S. NAVY

"For distinguished service in the line of his profession, as Commanding Officer, **USS ENTERPRISE,** when, on February 1, 1942 his ship was under a heavy bombing attack in enemy waters (near the Marshall Islands). By his courage and resourcefulness he saved his ship from serious damage."

CAPTAIN JAMES L. NEEFUS, U.S. NAVY

"For action during Japanese attacks on Midway Islands, December 7, 1941 to May 7, 1942. Captain James Neefus exhibited heroism and tenacity in pressing the aerial attack and skillful maneuvering of aircraft in attacks on enemy aircraft."

LIEUTENANT WILLIAM W. OUTERBRIDGE, U.S. NAVY

"As Command Officer of the destroyer **USS WARD,** Lieutenant Outerbridge conducted operations on patrol off the Pearl Harbor entrance which resulted in destruction of a Japanese submarine at 6:40 a.m., December 7, more than an hour before the attack on Pearl Harbor."

SEAMAN FIRST CLASS WILLIAM WHITEFORD PARKER, U.S. NAVY

"For devotion to duty, extraordinary courage and disregard of his own safety during the attack on the Fleet in Pearl Harbor, Territory of Hawaii, by Japanese forces, December 7, 1941. Despite orders from his gun captain to take cover, Seaman First Class Parker remained at his station on antiaircraft gun No. 1 with two other members of his gun crew until he was blown overboard by an explosion."

LIEUTENANT COMMANDER LEWIS S. PARKS, U.S.NAVY

"For distinguished service while engaged in hazardous submarine patrol

duties in own and enemy waters. Lieutenant Commander Parks commanded his crew and ship to successfully attack and destroy enemy ships."

CORPORAL DALE L. PETERS, U.S. MARINE CORPS

"For exceptionally meritorious service, extraordinary courage and disregard of his own condition during the bombardment of Sand Island, Midway Islands, by Japanese forces on December 7, 1941. Corporal Peters was
checking communications in an airplane hangar tower when he was blown
through a window by a shell blast. After a fall of fourteen feet, still dazed,
he rejoined his detail which was removing large aerial bombs from the burning hangar."

RADIOMAN SECOND CLASS ROBERT J. PETERSON, U.S. NAVY

"For distinguished service and devotion to duty when, promptly at the
onset of the first attack by Japanese planes on the Naval Air Station,
Kaneohe Bay, T.H., December 7, 1941, he secured and manned a machine-
gun mounted on an instruction stand in a completely exposed section of
airplane parking ramp under heavy enemy machinegun strafing fire. He
continued to return the enemy fire with telling effect during three enemy
strafing and bomb-attacks, with complete disregard for his own safety. Immediately following one attack he entered a group of blazing planes in which
ammunition and gasoline exploded violently. Without assistance he ex-
tinguished a serious fire in one plane, saving it from destruction. His extraordinary heroism and conduct in this action are considered to be in
keeping with the highest traditions of the Naval Service."

GUNNER JACKSON C. PHARRIS, U.S. NAVY

"For distinguished service in the line of his profession and for rescuing
personnel while attached to the **USS CALIFORNIA** during the Japanese
attack on Pearl Harbor, December 7, 1941. Though stunned and severely
injured by a torpedo which struck directly under his station, on his own
initiative he maintained an ammunition supply to anti-aircraft guns. Twice
rendered unconscious, and painfully injured he risked his life to drag unconscious shipmates to safety."
NOTE: This Navy Cross was upgraded to a Medal of Honor at a later date.

COMMANDER JOHN S. PHILLIPS, U.S. NAVY

"For distinguished service in line of his profession as Commanding Officer of the **USS NEOSHO** during the attack on the Fleet in Pearl Harbor, T.H., by Japanese forces on December 7, 1941. At the time of the attack the **USS NEOSHO** was moored alongside the gasoline dock, Naval Air Station, Pearl Harbor, and had just completed discharging gasoline at that station. When fire was opened on enemy planes, Commander Phillips realized the serious fire hazard of remaining alongside the dock as well as being in a position that prevented a battleship from getting underway, got underway immediately. Mooring lines were cut, and without the assistance of tugs, Commander Phillips accomplished the extremely difficult task of getting the ship underway from this particular berth in a most efficient manner, the difficulty being greatly increased by a battleship having capsized in the harbor."

LIEUTENANT COMMANDER CECIL D. RIGGS, MEDICAL CORPS, U.S. NAVY

"For distinguished service, extraordinary courage and disregard of his own safety during the attack on the Fleet in Pearl Harbor, T.H., by Japanese forces on December 7, 1941. Despite the severe enemy bombing and strafing of the Naval Air Station, Pearl Harbor, Lieutenant Commander Riggs, on duty at the time, immediately reorganized the medical facilities available to care for the many wounded men arriving at the station from the damaged ships. His excellent judgment, quick thinking and outstanding ability in the sudden emergency were in keeping with the best traditions of the Naval Service."

LIEUTENANT (jg) JAMES W. ROBB, Jr., U.S. NAVY

"For distinguished service in line of his profession, extraordinary courage and disregard of his own safety during the attack on the Fleet in Pearl Harbor, T.H., by Japanese forces on December 7, 1941. Although contact with the enemy meant almost certain destruction and despite the lack of any armament in this type plane, Lieutenant Robb voluntarily piloted a JRS amphibian plane, equipped only with Springfield rifles, in search for and to obtain information of the enemy forces."

RADIOMAN SECOND CLASS WILLIAM R. ROBERTS, U.S. NAVY

"For extraordinary courage and disregard of his own safety during the attack on the Fleet in Pearl Harbor, T.H., by Japanese forces on December 7, 1941. As radiomangunner of a battleship scout plane returning to Pearl Harbor after a search mission, he attempted to save the life of pilot, Lt.

(jg) J.B. Ginn, USN. Crashing eight miles offshore, both men were rendered unconscious. Roberts recovered and freed Ginn. Repeatedly diving, despite cuts and bruises, once almost drowning when he became entangled, he obtained the inflatable rubber life raft. He placed the unconscious Ginn on a wingfloat. Towing the pilot, he paddled to shore where a large breaker capsized the float. He located Ginn, who had been lost in the surf, dragged him ashore and started for aid. An Army patrol took them to a hospital where the pilot died. Roberts' lacerated head required fifteen stitches."

ENSIGN WESLEY H. RUTH, U.S. NAVY

"For distinguished service in line of his profession, extraordinary courage and disregard of his own safety during the attack on the Fleet in Pearl Harbor, T.H., by Japanese forces on December 7, 1941. Although contact with the enemy meant almost certain destruction and despite lack of armament in this type plane, Lt. Ruth voluntarily piloted a JRS amphibian plane, with only Springfield rifles, in search of and to obtain information of the enemy forces. At a point two hundred miles north of Oahu, Lt. Ruth did contact an enemy aircraft and only through prompt and extremely skillful handling of his plane did he succeed in escaping and returning to Pearl Harbor."

ENSIGN D. ARNOLD SINGLETON, U.S. NAVAL RESERVE

"For distinguished service in the line of his profession, extraordinary courage, and disregard of personal danger during the attack on the Fleet in Pearl Harbor, T.H., on December 7, 1941. As Fuel Officer of the Naval Air Station (Ford Island) Pearl Harbor, he had just completed fueling the station from **USS NEOSHO** which was moored at the gasoline dock, and was taking back suction to clean the lines when the first aerial attack started. Although under fire from the enemy, he continued with his duty, directing the removal of the hoses which enabled the **USS NEOSHO** to leave her berth, and personally supervised the opening of the sprinkler valves on the fuel tanks thereby rendering the gasoline supply of the station secure. Upon completion of these duties, despite very severe enemy bombing and strafing of the station, he turned his efforts to assisting in caring for the wounded men that were arriving at the station."

LIEUTENANT COMMANDER CHESTER C. SMITH, U.S. NAVY

"For extraordinary heroism and outstanding courage as Commanding Officer of a U.S. submarine engaged in war patrol. Despite the close watch maintained by enemy air and surface ship patrol, LCDR Smith boldly engaged the enemy in a daring attack which resulted in the sinking of the two largest vessels lying at anchor in closed waters. Again after contacting an escorted enemy vessel supply enemy forces, he closed range and promptly attacked the ship which was subsequently found to have been destroyed. Finally, a 3000 ton Japanese tanker was the last of eight enemy vessels to be destroyed by the submarine since the commencement of hostilities. LCDR Smith's fine qualities of inspiring leadership and the courageous, aggressive spirit of his command in offensive action were in keeping with the highest traditions of the United States Naval Service."

BOATSWAIN'S MATE SECOND CLASS HAROLD FRANCIS SMITH, U.S. NAVY

"For devotion to duty, extraordinary courage and complete disregard of his own safety during the attack on the Fleet at Pearl Harbor, T.H., December 7, 1941 by the Japanese forces. After the **USS ARIZONA** had been ordered abandoned, BM2c Smith unhesitatingly made repeated trips in a motor launch between her and an air station landing, carrying wounded, despite heavy bombardment and strafing, and blazing oil on the water, thereby saving many lives that would otherwise have been lost."

YEOMAN FIRST CLASS JAMES L. SNYDER, U.S. NAVY

"For extraordinary courage, initiative and disregard of his own safety during the attack by Japanese forces on the Fleet at Pearl Harbor, T.H., December 7, 1941. As phone-talker on the navigation bridge of the **USS NEVADA** he remained on the navigation bridge until forced by fire to leap to safety to the bridge below. Thence he went to an antiaircraft gun ammunition ready box and despite the fact that the heat was exploding other similar boxes, he removed all the ammunition thereby saving lives and assuring continuance of the gun's operation."

FIRST LIEUTENANT CHARLES W. SOMERS, Jr., U.S. MARINE CORPS

"For action during the Japanese attacks on Wake Island, December 7, 1941 to May 7, 1942."

ENSIGN JOSEPH K. TAUSSIG, Jr., U.S. NAVY

"For distinguished service in the line of his profession, extraordinary courage and disregard of his own physical condition during the attack on the Fleet in Pearl Harbor, T.H., by Japanese forces on December 7, 1941. As senior officer present in the anti-aircraft battery of the **USS NEVADA,** although seriously wounded, he refused to leave his battle station and insisted on continuing the control of his battery's fire until he was forcefully taken from his station and lowered in a stretcher, other means of descent being blocked by fire."

ENSIGN THOMAS H. TAYLOR, U.S. NAVY

"For distinguished service in line of his profession, extraordinary courage and disregard of his own condition during the attack on the Fleet in Pearl Harbor, T.H., by Japanese forces on December 7, 1941. Having assumed control of the port anti-aircraft battery of the **USS NEVADA,** he continued to direct efficiently that battery throughout the attack, although wounded by shell fragments, burned and deafened due to broken eardrums. His presence of mind in playing a hose on the ready ammunition boxes that were becoming very hot, due to the proximity of fires, prevented casualties and heavy damage to the battery."

ENSIGN PERRY L. TEAFF, U.S. NAVY

"For distinguished service in line of his profession, extraordinary courage and disregard of his own safety during the attack on the Fleet in Pearl Harbor, T.H., by Japanese forces on December 7, 1941. In order to search for and attack the enemy, Ensign Teaff unhesitatingly took off from the Naval Air Station, Ford Island, Pearl Harbor, in a plane which had already been damaged by enemy fire, and continued with a defective engine at a time when no chance for rescue existed."

AVIATION MACHINIST MATE SECOND CLASS ALBERT CURTIS THATCHER, U.S. NAVY

"For devotion to duty and disregard for his personal safety during the attack on the Fleet in Pearl Harbor, T.H., by Japanese forces on December 7, 1941. Wounded in the severe enemy bombing and strafing attack on the naval air station, Ford Island, Pearl Harbor, AMM2c Thatcher continued to assist Ensign D. Arnold Singleton, USNR, in securing fuel lines at the station and helping free the tanker, **USS NEOSHO** that was fueling the station."

LIEUTENANT COMMANDER FRANCIS J. THOMAS, U.S. NAVAL RESERVE

"For distinguished service in the line of his profession when as senior surviving officer aboard he took command of the **USS NEVADA** during the attack on the Fleet in Pearl Harbor, T.H., by Japanese forces on December 7, 1941, and despite severe enemy bombing and strafing at the time, handled it in an outstanding manner. Although the **USS NEVADA** had been torpedoed and bombed, he displayed excellent judgment in promptly getting the **USS NEVADA** underway and moving her from the proximity of the **USS ARIZONA** which was surrounded by burning oil and was afire from stem to stern. Furthermore, when the entire forward part of his ship was afire and it appeared that she might sink, as a result of further bombing, he ran her aground in order to save her."

ENSIGN ROBERT E. THOMAS, Jr., U.S. NAVY

"For distinguished service in the line of his profession, exceptional courage, coolness and devotion to duty during the attack on the Fleet in Pearl Harbor, T.H., by Japanese forces on December 7, 1941. Despite heavy bombing, strafing and torpedo attacks, Ensign Thomas, battery officer on the five-inch anti-aircraft battery of the **USS NEVADA,** although seriously wounded and handicapped by heavy casualties to the personnel of the battery, maintained a highly effective fire from his battery."

FIREMAN SECOND CLASS JOHN BARTH VAESSEN, U.S. NAVAL RESERVE

"For devotion to duty and disregard for his personal safety during the attack on the Fleet in Pearl Harbor, T.H., by Japanese forces on December 7, 1941. Although realizing that his ship, the **USS UTAH,** was capsizing, F2c Vaessen remained at his post at the forward distribution board after word had been passed to abandon ship, and kept the lights burning as long as possible. Trapped, he later was rescued through a hole cut in the bottom of the capsized target ship."

LIEUTENANT COMMANDER WILLIAM F. VERDEN, U.S. NAVY

"For his participation February 1, 1942, in the attack on the Marshall Islands."

AVIATION MACHINIST MATE LEONARD H. WAGONER, U.S. NAVY

"For extraordinary heroism on December 30, 1941, in rescuing crew of nine men and officers of Army B17 forced down at sea four days previously. In that Leonard H.Wagoner, Aviation Machinist's Mate first class, USN, on Dec. 30, 1941, while acting as second pilot of a patrol plane at a very great distance from land, sighted two life rafts and, after the sea had been reported as too rough to attempt a rescue, did assist his patrol plane commander, Ens. F. M. Fisler, in a very rough sea, rescuing the crew, nine officers and men, of an Army B-17 forced down at sea on December 26, 1941, and did thereby exhibit rare vigilance, skill and extraordinary heroism above and beyond the normal demands of duty, the United States then being in a state of war."

LIEUTENANT COMMANDER FREDERICK B. WARDER, USN

"As commanding officer of submarine **USS SEAWOLF,** Lieutenant Commander Warder successfully operated his ship in Pacific waters where he sank or damaged eight Japanese ships during the first few months of WW II."

LIEUTENANT COMMANDER DAVID CHARLES WHITE, USN

"For distinguished service in line of his profession as commanding officer of **USS PLUNGER,** while on hazardous submarine patrol duty in own and enemy waters. Despite intensive enemy air and surface antisubmarine patrols, Lieutenant Commander White successfully attacked and sank an enemy vessel of 7,000 tons. During the period of this patrol a total of twenty-four depth charges were dropped around and near **USS PLUNGER.** In spite of this, LCDR White's assignment was completed without damage to his submarine or injury to the personnel under his command."

NOTE: In lieu of a second NAVY CROSS, the President of the United States presented a Gold Star to LCDR White. The Citation follows:

"For extrordinary heroism and distinguished service as Commanding Officer of a submarine in offensive action against enemy Japanese forces during the period from May 27 to July 15, 1942. Availing himself of every attack opportunity while conducting hazardous submarine patrol operations in enemy-controlled waters, LCDR White followed a persistently aggressive course and succeeded in sinking a total of 18,000 tons of enemy shipping, and, in addition, inflicted severe damage on a total of 10,000 tons without injury or damage to material or personnel of his command. In the superb handling of his vessel and in his gallant and intrepid leadership, LCDR White sustained and enhanced the finest traditions of the United States Naval Service."

LIEUTENANT COMMANDER CHARLES W. WILKENS, USN

"For his participation February 1, 1942 in the attack on the Marshall Islands. For distinguished duty in the line of his profession as Commanding Officer of submarine **USS NARWHAL** in aggressive and successful action against the enemy during the period February 2 to March 28, 1942, while engaged in hazardous submarine patrol in enemy waters. Despite intensive enemy surface patrols, he sank 12,000 tons of enemy merchant shipping without damage or injury to material or personnel of his command."

* Posthumous award

Distinguished Service Cross

DISTINGUISHED SERVICE CROSS

CRITERIA FOR DISTINGUISHED SERVICE CROSS
(This Army Medal rates equal with the Navy Cross.)

The Distinguished Service Cross is awarded by the President or in the name of the President, to any person, who, while serving in any capacity in the Armed services, shall distinguish himself by extraordinary heroism in connection with military operations against an armed enemy of the United States, under circumstances not justifying the award of the Medal of Honor.

DESCRIPTION

The decoration consists of a cross of bronze, the ends being elaborated. An eagle on a wreath which is tied with a ribbon bearing the words FOR VALOR is surmounted on the cross. The reverse bears a panel for appropriate inscription.

The ribbon is navy blue bordered with thin stripes of white and broader stripes of red.

DISTINGUISHED SERVICE CROSS RECIPIENTS

ANDERSON, Sergeant LeRoy, U.S.Army
*ANDERSON, Corporal William T., Army Air Corps, U.S. Army
ASHLEY, Private First Class Early D., Army Air Corps
*BARNICLE, Second Lieutenant Gerald J., Army Air Corps
*BATTAGLIE, Staff Sergeant Salvatore, Army Air Corps
COLLINS, Captain James F., Army Air Corps
*DECKER, Staff Sergeant Richard C., Army Air Corps
DUNN, Sergeant Jack D., Army Air Corps
FENNO, Lieutenant Commander Frank W., U.S. Navy
GOGOJ, Staff Sergeant John J., Army Air Corps
*HARGIS, Second Lieutenant William D. Hargis, Army Air Corps
*HUFFSTICKLER, Private Benjamin, Army Air Corps
JOHNSEN, Second Lieutenant Russell H., Army Air Corps
JOYCE, Corporal John D., Army Air Corps

*KIMMEY, Staff Sergeant Doyle, 19th Transport Squadron, U.S. Army
LeFLEUR, Chaplain Padre Joseph, U.S. Army
*MAYES, First Lieutenant Herbert C., Army Air Corps
*McALLISTER, Second Lieutenant Garrett H., 18th Reconnaissance Squadron (M) Army Air Corps
MELO, Corporal Frank L., 18th Reconnaissance Squadron (M), Army Air Corps
MOHON, Sergeant Ernest M. Jr., Headquarters and Headquarters Squadron, 5th Bombardment Group, (H) Army Air Corps
MOORE, First Lieutenant Pren L., 18th Reconnaissance Squadron (M), Army Air Corps
MOORE, Second Lieutenant William W., 18th Reconnaissance Squadron (M), Army Air Corps
MURI, First Lieutenant James P., 18th Reconnaissance Squadron (M), Army Air Corps
*OWEN, Sergeant Albert E., 69th Bombardment Squadron (M), Army Air Corps
*SEITZ, Corporal Bernard C., 69th Bombardment Squadron (M), Army Air Corps
*SCHUMAN, Second Lieutenant John P., 69th Bombardment Squadron (M), Army Air Corps
TAYLOR, Second Lieutenant Kenneth Marlar, Army Air Corps
TRAPNELL, Major Thomas J.H., U.S. Army Cavalry
*VIA, Sergeant James E., 394th Bombardment Squadron (H), Army Air Corps
VILLINES, Second Lieutenant Colin O., 69th Bombardment Squadron (M), Army Air Corps
*WALTERS, Private Roy W., 18th Reconnaissance Squadron (M), Army Air Corps
*WATSON, Second Lieutenant William S., 69th Bombardment Squadron (M), Army Air Corps
WEEMS, Second Lieutenant Thomas N. Jr., 69th Bombardment Squadron (M), Army Air Corps
WELCH, Second Lieutenant George Schwarz, Army Air Corps
WHITE, Technical Sergeant Raymond S., 69th Bombardment Squadron (M), Army Air Corps
*WITTINGTON, Second Lieutenant Leonard H., 69th Bombardment Squadron, Army Air Corps

* Posthumous Award

DISTINGUISHED SERVICE CROSS

SERGEANT LEROY C. ANDERSON, U.S. ARMY

"For destroying Japanese machinegun nests with a small group of tanks deploying through heavy jungle country. When his tank was demolished his crew proceeded on foot and continued to fight with rifles and hand grenades. His action enabled U.S. Infantry to advance and reestablish a broken line on the Bataan Peninsula during the early months of the war."

*CORPORAL WILLIAM T. ANDERSON, ARMY AIR CORPS, 24th DIVISION, U.S. ARMY

"For extraordinary heroism during the Japanese attack on Hickam Field, Territory of Hawaii, 7 December 1941. While on duty as a radio operator Corporal Anderson voluntarily obtained a sub-machine gun and with utter disregard for his own safety took position in the open field without cover and continued to fire at enemy planes which were bombing and strafing the field, until he was mortally wounded."

PRIVATE FIRST CLASS EARLY D. ASHLEY, ARMY AIR CORPS, U.S. ARMY

"For extraordinary heroism in action near Midway Island, 4 June 1942. Private First Class Ashley, as a gunner of a medium bombardment airplane, displayed extraordinary heroism during an extremely hazardous and difficult torpedo-bombing mission against the Japanese Navy. He served his gun against strong fighter opposition until seriously wounded by enemy fire, and after being wounded continued to assist another crew member in serving the gun until enemy opposition had ceased."

*SECOND LIEUTENANT GERALD J. BARNICLE, ARMY AIR CORPS, U.S. ARMY

"For extraordinary heroism in action near Midway Island, 4 June 1942. Lieutenant Barnicle, as bombardier and gunner of a medium bombardment airplane, displayed extraordinary heroism during a torpedo-bombing mission against the Japanese Navy. The success of the mission was dependent entirely upon the skill, courageousness and unfaltering devotion to duty of the crew members of the airplanes participating, who unhesitatingly entered into the attack at great personal risk to their own lives in the face of concentrated gunfire of the Japanese Naval forces and fighter planes. During this, the first torpedo attack ever carried out by the Army Air Forces, the airplane on which Lieutenant Barnicle was gunner and bombardier, was lost."

*STAFF SERGEANT SALVATORE BATTAGLIA, ARMY AIR CORPS, U.S. ARMY

"For extraordinary heroism in action near Midway Island, 4 June 1942. Staff Sergeant Battaglia, as aerial engineer and gunner of a medium bombardment airplane, displayed extraordinary heroism during a torpedo-bombing mission against the Japanese Navy. The success of the mission was dependent entirely upon the skill, courageousness and unfaltering devotion to duty of the crew members of the airplanes participating, who unhesitatingly entered into the attack at great personal risk to their own lives in the face of concentrated gunfire of the Japanese Naval forces and fighter planes. During this, the first torpedo attack ever carried out by the Army Air Forces, the airplane on which Staff Sergeant Battaglia was aerial engineer and gunner, was lost."

CAPTAIN JAMES F. COLLINS, ARMY AIR CORPS, U.S. ARMY

"For extraordinary heroism in action near Midway Island, 4 June 1942. Capt. Collins led a provisional flight of medium bombardment airplanes to seek out and attack a large Japanese Naval Force. Upon sighting the enemy fleet, he unswervingly led his airplanes into action. Subjected immediately to an exceptionally strong fighter attack with which he had a running gun fight for almost thirty minutes, it was only by skillful handling of his airplane that he was able to avoid this and subsequent anti-aircraft fire and keep the formation together. Arriving before other Army forces, he carried out the first torpedo attack ever entered into by airplanes of this type or by the Army Air Forces, and its ultimate success primarily depended upon the skill and intrepidity of the leader. Capt. Collins sought out a large enemy aircraft carrier protected on all sides by gunfire of all types from enemy battleships, cruisers and destroyers. Although the carrier was trying to elude his approach, he did, by evasive maneuvering, avoid the gunfire and completed his approach. By his superior leadership Capt. Collins carried out a most hazardous mission under the most adverse conditions and was unfaltering in his courage."

*STAFF SERGEANT RICHARD C. DECKER, ARMY AIR CORPS, U.S. ARMY

"For extraordinary heroism in action near Midway Island, 4 June 1942. Staff Sergeant Decker, an aerial engineer and gunner of a medium bombardment airplane, displayed extraordinary heroism during a torpedo bombing mission against the Japanese Navy. The success of the mission was dependent entirely upon the skill, courageousness and unfaltering devotion to duty of the crew members of the airplanes participating, who unhesitatingly entered into the attack at great personal risk to their own lives in the face of concentrated gunfire of the Japanese Naval forces and fighter planes. During this, the first torpedo attack ever carried out by the Army Air Forces, the airplane on which Staff Sergeant Decker was aerial engineer and gunner, was lost."

SERGEANT JACK D. DUNN, ARMY AIR CORPS, U.S. ARMY

"For extraordinary heroism in action near Midway Island, 4 June 1942. Sergeant Dunn, as aerial engineer and gunner of a medium bombardment airplane, participated in an extremely hazardous and difficult torpedo-bombing mission against the Japanese Navy. He displayed extraordinary heroism throughout the attack in fighting off many enemy fighters during and after the attack. By his skilled airmanship and courageousness he materially aided in the success of the first torpedo attack ever carried out by the Army Air Forces."

LIEUTENANT COMMANDER FRANK W. FENNO, U.S. NAVY

"For extraordinary heroism while operating his submarine in enemy-controlled waters during January-March 1942 in the performance of an unusual and hazardous mission for the War Department. Carrying a heavy load of antiaircraft ammunition urgently needed by the beleaguered forces of General Douglas MacArthur in the Philippine Islands, the USS TROUT departed from Pearl Harbor, T.H. for Corregidor Island, Manila Bay, at 0900, 12 January 1942, refueling at Midway Island on 16 January 1942. The TROUT proceeded on the surface until 21 January, travelling submerged thereafter during daylight hours. At 0230, 27 January 1942, an unsuccessful night attack was made on a lighted enemy vessel, resulting in the TROUT being chased by the vessel at such speed as to force the TROUT to dive in order to escape. On 3 February 1942, after dark, the TROUT made rendezvous off Corregidor with an escort motor torpedo boat. The TROUT then followed the escort at high speed through a winding passage in a mine field to South Dock, Corregidor Island, where she unloaded 3500 rounds of antiaircraft artillery ammunition for the Army Forces defending Bataan Peninsula and Corregidor. Twenty tons of gold and silver, securities, diplomatic and United States mail and two additional torpedoes were loaded on the **TROUT** for the return voyage. The **TROUT** cleared the Corregidor dock at 0400, 4 February, and bottomed in Manila Bay during daylight 4 February. Surfacing that night, additional securities and mail were loaded before the **TROUT** departed from Manila Bay through the mine field. On the return trip one enemy merchant vessel and one patrol vessel were attacked and sunk. The **TROUT** arrived at Pearl Harbor 3 March 1942 after 51 days at sea. Lieutenant Commander Fenno's example of fearlessness, zeal and devotion to duty resulted in the accomplishment of a mission of great service to the Army (sic) of the United States."

STAFF SERGEANT JOHN J. GOGOJ, ARMY AIR CORPS, U.S. ARMY

"For extraordinary heroism in action near Midway Island, 4 June 1942. Staff Sergeant Gogoj, as aerial engineer and gunner of a medium bombardment airplane, participated in an extremely hazardous and difficult torpedo-bombing mission against the Japanese Navy. He displayed extraordinary heroism during the mission by fighting off enemy fighters and although he incurred painful head wounds during the attack, continued to operate his guns until free of enemy opposition. By his skilled airmanship and courageousness he was instrumental in the success of the first torpedo attack ever carried out by the Army Air Forces."

*SECOND LIEUTENANT WILLIAM D. HARGIS, Jr., ARMY AIR CORPS, U.S. ARMY

"For extraordinary heroism in action near Midway Island, 4 June 1942. Lieutenant Hargis, as navigator of a medium bombardment airplane, displayed extraordinary heroism during a torpedo-bombing mission against the Japanese Navy. The success of the mission was dependent entirely upon the skill, courageousness and unfaltering devotion to duty of the crew members of the airplanes participating, who unhesitatingly entered into the attack at great personal risk to their own lives in the face of concentrated gunfire of the Japanese Naval forces and fighter planes. During this, the first torpedo attack ever carried out by the Army Air Forces, the airplane on which Lieutenant Hargis was navigator, was lost."

*PRIVATE BENJAMIN F. HUFFSTICKLER, ARMY AIR CORPS, U.S. ARMY

"For extraordinary heroism in action near Midway Island, 4 June 1942. Private Huffstickler, as radioman and gunner of a medium bombardment airplane, displayed extraordinary heroism during a torpedo-bombing mission against the Japanese Navy. The success of the mission was dependent entirely upon the skill, courageousness and unfaltering devotion to duty of the crew members of the airplanes participating, who unhesitatingly entered into the attack at great personal risk to their own lives in the face of concentrated gunfire of the Japanese Naval forces and fighter planes. During this, the first torpedo attack ever carried out by the Army Air Forces the airplane on which Private Huffstickler was radioman and gunner, was lost."

SECOND LIEUTENANT RUSSELL H. JOHNSEN, ARMY AIR CORPS, U.S. ARMY

"For extraordinary heroism in action near Midway Island, 4 June 1942. Lieutenant Johnsen, as bombardier and gunner of a medium bombardment airplane, displayed extraordinary heroism during an extremely hazardous and difficult torpedo-bombing mission against the Japanese Navy. His skill and courageousness in operating his gun in the face of superior fighter opposition and intense anti-aircraft fire was instrumental in the success of the first torpedo attack ever carried out by the Army Air Forces."

CORPORAL JOHN D. JOYCE, ARMY AIR CORPS, U.S. ARMY

"For extraordinary heroism in action near Midway Island, 4 June 1942. Corporal Joyce, as gunner of a medium bombardment airplane, displayed extraordinary heroism during an extremely hazardous and difficult torpedo-bombing mission against the Japanese Navy. By his skill and courageousness in the face of a heavy enemy fighter and anti-aircraft opposition, he aided materially in the success of the first torpedo attack ever carried out by the Army Air Forces."

*STAFF SERGEANT DOYLE KIMMEY, 19th TRANSPORT SQUADRON, ARMY AIR CORPS, U.S. ARMY

"For extraordinary heroism during the Japanese air attack on Hickam Field, Territory of Hawaii, 7 December 1941. While on duty as an aerial engineer, Sergeant Kimmey voluntarily obtained a submachine gun, took cover under a small truck, and opened fire at the low-flying enemy planes which were bombing and strafing the area. When his supply of ammunition was exhausted Sergeant Kimmey courageously left his shelter during the heavy attack to retrieve an abandoned sub-machine gun with a supply of ammunition and after gaining his former position resumed fire until the truck under which he was taking cover was directly hit by a bomb resulting in his instant death."

CHAPLAIN PADRE JOSEPH F. LeFLEUR, U.S. ARMY

"During the first Japanese attack on a Phillippine Island airport on December 8, 1941, Chaplain LeFleur worked among the wounded, removing them to safety, and comforting the dying."

*FIRST LIEUTENANT HERBERT C. MAYES, ARMY AIR CORPS, U.S. ARMY

"For extraordinary heroism in action near Midway Island, 4 June 1942. Lieutenant Mayes, as pilot of a medium bombardment airplane, displayed extraordinary heroism during a torpedo-bombing mission against the Japanese Navy. The success of the mission was dependent entirely upon the skill, courageousness and unfaltering devotion to duty of crew members of the airplanes participating, who unhesitatingly entered into the attack at great personal risk to their lives in the face of concentrated gunfire of Japanese Naval forces and fighter planes. During this, the first torpedo attack ever carried out by Army Air Forces, the airplane on which Lieutenant Mayes was pilot, was lost."

*SECOND LIEUTENANT GARRET H. McCALLISTER, 18th RECONNAISSANCE SQUADRON (M) ARMY AIR CORPS, U.S. ARMY

"For extraordinary heroism in action near Midway Island, 4 June 1942. Lieutenant McCallister, as co-pilot of a medium bombardment airplane, displayed extraordinary heroism during a torpedo-bombing mission against the Japanese Navy. The success of the mission was dependent entirely upon the skill, courageousness and unfaltering devotion to duty of the crew members of the airplanes participating, who unhesitatingly entered into the attack at great personal risk to their lives in the face of concentrated gunfire of Japanese Naval forces and fighter planes. During this, the first torpedo attack ever carried out by Army Air Forces, the airplane on which Lieutenant McCallister was co-pilot was lost."

CORPORAL FRANK L. MELO, 18th RECONNAISSANCE SQUAD-RON (M), ARMY AIR CORPS, U.S. ARMY

"For extraordinary heroism in action near Midway Island, 4 June 1942. Corporal Melo, as radioman and gunner of a medium bombardment airplane, displayed extraordinary heroism during an extremely hazardous and difficult torpedo-bombing mission against the Japanese Navy. Although wounded during the attack, he carried on with his duties and by skilled airmanship and courageousness materially aided in the success of the first torpedo attack ever carried out by the Army Air Forces."

SERGEANT ERNEST M MOHON, Jr., HEADQUARTERS AND HEADQUARTERS SQUADRON, 5th BOMBARDMENT GROUP (H), ARMY AIR CORPS, U.S. ARMY

"For extraordinary heroism in action near Midway Island, 4 June 1942. Sergeant Mohon, as bombardier and gunner of a medium bombardment airplane, displayed extraordinary heroism during an extremely hazardous and difficult torpedo-bombing mission against the Japanese Navy. His skill and courageousness in operating his gun in the face of superior fighter op-position and intense anti-aircraft fire was instrumental in the success of the first torpedo attack ever carried out by the Army Air Forces."

FIRST LIEUTENANT PREN L. MOORE, 18th RECONNAISSANCE SQUADRON (M), ARMY AIR CORPS, U.S. ARMY

"For extraordinary heroism in action near Midway Island, 4 June 1942. Lieutenant Moore, as co-pilot of a medium bombardment plane, par-ticipated in an extremely hazardous and difficult torpedo-bombing mis-sion against the Japanese Navy. He displayed extraordinary heroism throughout the attack by leaving his station as co-pilot to administer to wounds of three other crew members and by manning a gun position whose gunner had been totally disabled and fighting off enemy fighters. By his skilled airmanship and courageousness while subject to intense fighter and anti-aircraft opposition, he was instrumental in the success of the first torpedo attack ever carried out by the Army Air Forces."

SECOND LIEUTENANT WILLIAM W. MOORE, 18th RECON-NAISSANCE SQUADRON (M), ARMY AIR CORPS, U.S. ARMY

"For extraordinary heroism in action near Midway Island, 4 June 1942. Lieutenant Moore, as navigator of a medium bombardment airplane, displayed extraordinary heroism during an extremely hazardous and difficult torpedo-bombing mission against the Japanese Navy. By his airmanship, skill in his specialty and courageousness he successfully navigated his airplane in seeking out the enemy and in returning to his base through superior and intense fighter and anti-aircraft opposition, thereby materially aiding in the success of the first torpedo attack ever carried out by the Army Air Forces."

FIRST LIEUTENANT JAMES P. MURI, 18th RECONNAISSANCE SQUADRON (M), ARMY AIR CORPS, U.S. ARMY

"For extraordinary heroism in action near Midway Island, 4 June 1942. Lieutenant Muri, as pilot of a medium bombardment airplane, participated in an extremely hazardous and difficult torpedo-bombing mission against the Japanese Navy. He displayed extraordinary heroism and courageousness in maneuvering his airplane to secure the maximum effectiveness of his torpedo in the face of superior enemy fighter and anti-aircraft opposition, and was highly instrumental in the success of the first torpedo attack ever carried out by the Army Air Forces."

*SERGEANT ALBERT E. OWEN, 69th BOMBARDMENT SQUADRON (M) ARMY AIR CORPS, U.S. ARMY

"For extraordinary heroism in action near Midway Island, 4 June 1942. Sergeant Owen, as radioman and gunner of a medium bombardment airplane, displayed extraordinary heroism during a torpedo-bombing mission against the Japanese Navy. The success of the mission was dependent entirely upon the skill, courageousness and unfaltering devotion to duty of the crew members of the airplanes participating, who unhesitatingly entered into the attack at great personal risk to their lives in the face of concentrated gunfire of Japanese Naval forces and fighter planes. During this, the first torpedo attack ever carried out by the Army Air Force, the airplane on which Sergeant Owen was radioman and gunner, was lost."

*CORPORAL BERNARD C. SEITZ, 69th BOMBARDMENT SQUADRON (M), ARMY AIR CORPS, U.S. ARMY

"For extraordinary heroism in action near Midway Island, 4 June 1942. Corporal Seitz, as gunner of a medium bombardment airplane, displayed extraordinary heroism during a torpedo-bombing mission against the Japanese Navy. The success of the mission was dependent entirely upon the skill, courageousness and unfaltering devotion to duty of the crew members of the airplanes participating, who unhesitatingly entered into the attack at great personal risk to their lives in the face of concentrated gunfire of the Japanese Naval forces and fighter planes. During this, the first torpedo attack ever carried out by the Army Air Forces, the airplane on which Corporal Seitz was gunner, was lost."

*SECOND LIEUTENANT JOHN P. SCHUMAN, 69th BOMBARD-MENT SQUADRON (M), ARMY AIR CORPS, U.S. ARMY

"For extraordinary heroism during a torpedo-bombing mission against the Japanese Navy, in action near Midway Island, 4 June 1942, as navigator of a medium bombardment airplane. The success of the mission was dependent entirely upon the skill, courageousness and unfaltering devotion to duty of the crew members of the airplanes participating, who unhesitatingly entered into the attack at great personal risk to their lives in the face of concentrated gunfire of Japanese Navy forces and fighter planes. During this, the first torpedo attack ever carried out by the Army Air Forces, the airplane on which Lieutenant Schuman was navigator, was lost."

SECOND LIEUTENANT KENNETH MARLAR TAYLOR, UNITED STATES ARMY

"For extraordinary heroism in action over the Island of Oahu, T.H., and waters adjacent thereto, December 7, 1941. When surprised by a heavy air attack by Japanese forces on Wheeler Field and vicinity at approximately 8 a.m., he left Wheeler Field and proceeded by automobile under fire, to Haleiwa Landing Field, a distance of approximately ten miles, where the planes of his squadron were stationed. He immediately, on his own initiative, took off for the purpose of attacking the invading forces, without first obtaining information as to the number or type of planes in attacking forces, and proceeded to his initial point over Barbers Point. At take-off time his plane was equipped with thirty-caliber machineguns only. Upon arrival over Barbers Point, he observed a formation of approximately twelve planes over Ewa, about 1,000 feet below and ten miles away. Accompanied by only one other pursuit plane, he immediately attacked this enemy formation and shot down two enemy planes. No more enemy planes in sight, he proceeded to Wheeler to refuel and replenish ammunition. Reloading completed, but ammunition boxes not removed, a second wave of enemy planes attacked, approaching directly toward him at low altitude. Although advised not to go up again, Taylor made a quick take-off ending in a chandelle, thereby saving his plane as he escaped from a superior force of eight to ten planes by climbing into clouds. Lieutenant Taylor's initiative, presence of mind, coolness under fire against overwhelming odds in his first battle, expert maneuvering of his plane, and determined action contributed to a large extent toward driving off this sudden, unexpected attack."

MAJOR THOMAS J. H. TRAPNELL, U.S. ARMY CAVALRY

"For extraordinary heroism during action in the Philippine Islands, December 22, 1942, while U.S. cavalry engaged in rear guard action. During a concentration of enemy fire from tanks and infantry, Major Trapnell remained between the hostile forces and his own troops and set on fire a truck on a bridge somewhere in Launion Province. Then he waited calmly until the bridge had burned before leaving in a scout car to rejoin his troops."

*SERGEANT JAMES E. VIA, 394th BOMBARDMENT SQUADRON (H), ARMY AIR CORPS, U.S. ARMY

"For extraordinary heroism in action near Midway Island, 4 June 1942. Sergeant Via, as bombardier and gunner of a medium bombardment airplane, displayed extraordinary heroism during a torpedo-bombing mission against the Japanese Navy. The success of the mission was dependent entirely upon the skill, courageousness, and unfaltering devotion to duty of the crew members of the airplanes participating who unhesitatingly entered into the attack at great personal risk to their own lives in the face of concentrated gunfire of the Japanese Naval forces and fighter planes. During this, the first torpedo attack ever carried out by the Army Air Forces, the airplane on which Sergeant Via was bombardier and gunner, was lost."

SECOND LIEUTENANT COLIN O. VILLINES, 69th BOMBARDMENT SQUADRON (M), ARMY AIR CORPS, U.S. ARMY

"For extraordinary heroism in action near Midway Island, 4 June 1942. Lieutenant Villines, as co-pilot of a medium bombardment airplane, participated in an extremely hazardous and difficult torpedo-bombing mission against the Japanese Navy. He displayed extraordinary heroism throughout the attack, and by his skilled airmanship and courageousness while subjected to intense fighter and anti-aircraft opposition, he was instrumental in the success of the first torpedo attack ever carried out by the Army Air Force."

*PRIVATE ROY W. WALTERS, 18th RECONNAISSANCE SQUAD-RON (M), ARMY AIR CORPS, U.S. ARMY

"For extraordinary heroism in action near Midway Island, 4 June 1942. Private Walters, as gunner of a medium bombardment airplane, displayed extraordinary heroism during a torpedo-bombing mission against the Japanese Navy. The success of the mission was dependent entirely upon the skill, courageousness and unfaltering devotion to duty of the crew members of the airplanes participating, who unhesitatingly entered into the attack at great personal risk to their own lives in the face of concentrated gunfire of the Japanese Naval forces and fighter planes. During this, the first torpedo attack ever carried out by the Army Air Forces, the airplane on which Private Walters was gunner, was lost."

*SECOND LIEUTENANT WILLIAM S. WATSON, 69th BOM-BARDMENT SQUADRON (M), ARMY AIR CORPS, U.S. ARMY

"For extraordinary heroism in action near Midway Island, 4 June 1942. Lieutenant Watson, as pilot of a medium bombardment airplane, displayed extraordinary heroism during a torpedo-bombing mission against the Japanese Navy. The success of the mission was dependent entirely upon the skill, courageousness and unfaltering devotion to duty of the crew members of the airplanes participating, who unhesitatingly entered into the attack at great personal risk to their own lives in the face of concentrated gunfire of the Japanese Naval forces and fighter planes. During this, the first torpedo attack ever carried out by the Army Air Forces, the airplane on which Private Walters was gunner, was lost."

SECOND LIEUTENANT THOMAS N. WEEMS, JR., 69th BOM-BARDMENT SQUADRON (M), ARMY AIR CORPS, U.S. ARMY

"For extraordinary heroism in action near Midway Island, 4 June 1942. Second Lieutenant Weems, as navigator of a medium bombardment airplane, displayed extraordinary heroism during an extremely hazardous and difficult torpedo-bombing mission against the Japanese Navy. By his airmanship, skill in his specialty and courageousness, he successfully navigated his airplane in seeking out the enemy and in returning to his base through superior and intense fighter and anti-aircraft opposition, thereby materially aiding in the success of the first torpedo attack ever carried out by the Army Air Forces."

SECOND LIEUTENANT GEORGE SCHWARTZ WELCH, ARMY AIR CORPS, U.S. ARMY

"For extraordinary heroism in action over the Island of Oahu, T.H. and waters adjacent thereto, December 7, 1941. When surprised by a heavy air attack by Japanese forces on Wheeler Field and vicinity at approximately 8 a.m., he left Wheeler and proceeded by car, under fire, to Haleiwa Landing Field, approximately ten miles distance, where his squadron's planes were stationed. Immediately, on his own initiative, he took off for the purpose of attacking invading forces, without first obtaining information as to number or type of Japanese in the attacking force, and proceeded to his initial point over Barbers Point. At time of take off he was armed only with thirty-caliber machine guns. Upon arrival over Barbers Point, he observed a formation of approximately twelve planes over Ewa, about 100 feet below and ten miles away. Accompanied by only one other pursuit ship, he immediately attacked this enemy formation, shooting down an enemy dive bomber with one burst from three .30-caliber guns. At this point one .30 gun jammed. While engaged in this combat, his plane was hit by an incendiary bullet which passed through the baggage compartment just in rear of his seat. He climbed above the clouds, checked his plane, returned to the attack over Barbers Point and immediately attacked a Japanese plane running out to sea, which he shot down, the plane falling in the ocean. No more enemy planes in sight, he proceeded to Wheeler to refuel and replenish ammunition. Refueling and reloading completed but before repairing guns, a second wave of about fifteen enemy planes approached low over Wheeler. Three came at him and he immediately took off, headed straight into the attack and went to the assistance of a brother officer being attacked from the rear. This enemy plane burst into flames and crashed halfway between Wahiawa and Haleiwa. During this combat his plane was struck by three bullets from the rear gun of the ship he was attacking, one striking his motor, one the propeller and one the cowling. This attack wave having disappeared he returned to the vicinity of Ewa and found one enemy plane proceeding seaward, which he pursued and shot down about five miles off shore, immediately thereafter returning to his station at Haleiwa Landing Field. Lieutenant Welch's initiative, presence of mind, coolness under fire against overwhelming odds in his first battle, expert maneuvering of his plane, and determined action contributed to a large extent toward driving off this sudden unexpected enemy air attack."

TECHNICAL SERGEANT RAYMOND S. WHITE, 69th BOMBARDMENT SQUADRON (M), ARMY AIR CORPS, U.S. ARMY

"For extraordinary heroism in action near Midway Island, 4 June 1942. Technical Sergeant White, radioman and gunner of a medium bombardment airplane, displayed extraordinary heroism during an extremely hazardous and difficult torpedo-bombing mission against the Japanese Navy. By skilled airmanship and courageousness he was instrumental in the success of the first torpedo attack ever carried out by the Army Air Forces, in the face of intense enemy fighter and anti-aircraft opposition."

*SECOND LIEUTENANT LEONARD H. WHITTINGTON, 69th BOMBARDMENT SQUARDON (M), ARMY AIR CORPS, U.S. ARMY

"For extraordinary heroism in action near Midway Island, 4 June 1942. Lt. Whittington, co-pilot of a medium bombardment airplane, displayed extraordinary heroism during a torpedo-bombing mission against the Japanese Navy. The success of the mission was dependent entirely upon the skill, courageousness and unfaltering devotion to duty of the crew members of the airplanes participating, who unhesitatingly entered into the attack at great personal risk to their own lives in the face of concentrated gunfire of the Japanese Naval forces and fighter planes. During this, the first torpedo attack ever carried out by the Army Air Forces, the airplane on which Lieutenant Whittington was co-pilot, was lost."

* Posthumous awards

Army Distinguished Service Medal

THE ARMY DISTINGUISHED SERVICE MEDAL

The Army Distinguished Service Medal is awarded by the President to any person who, while serving in any capacity with the Army, shall hereafter distinguish himself or herself by exceptionally meritorious service to the Government in a duty of great responsibility in time of war in connection with military operations against an armed enemy of the United States.

DESCRIPTION

The bronze medal shows on its obverse the American coat of arms, pierced and mounted on a ribbon, on the upper part of which are the words FOR DISTINGUISHED SERVICE. The reverse shows the flags of the allies surrounded by various devices symbolic of the military activity. The ribbon is white with red and blue border stripes, the red on the outside.

Only one Army Distinguished Service Medal was awarded for action on December 7, 1941 and the following seven months.

LOCKARD, PRIVATE JOSEPH, U.S. ARMY

"For exceptionally meritorious service in a duty of great responsibility, when in charge of the detector unit operated by his organization, the Signal Aircraft Warning Regiment stationed on the Island of Oahu.

"In order that instruction in the operation of aircraft warning equipment might be given to another soldier under training, he, in devotion to duty, remained at his station upon completion of the scheduled operating period. At approximately 7:02 a.m. a signal was detected on the instruments, which, in the opinion of Lockard, signified a large number of planes in flight approximately 132 miles distant.

"At that moment Lockard was placed in a position of great and grave responsibility to his country. After rechecking the distance and azimuth Lockard promptly contacted the duty officer of the information center and furnished him with complete particulars of the readings.

"Subsequent investigations have proven conclusively that the airplanes reported by Lockard were the large Japanese air force which attacked the island of Oahu at approximately 7:55 a.m."

Navy Distinguished Service Medal

THE NAVY DISTINGUISHED SERVICE MEDAL

The President is authorized to present this medal to any person who, while in the naval service of the United States distinguishes himself by exceptionally meritorious service to the Government in a duty of great responsibility.

DESCRIPTION

The obverse of the medal contains an eagle displayed with wings reversed surrounded by a blue enameled circle containing the words UNITED STATES OF AMERICA. Surmounting the disk is a white enameled star with anchor in center. The reverse contains in the inner circle a vertical trident with a wreath on either side. Surrounding this is a circle containing the words FOR DISTINGUISHED SERVICE. The outer circle on both sides contains a rope. The bronze medal is suspended from a ribbon of dark blue with a yellow stripe in the center.

BROWN, Rear Admiral Wilson, Jr., U.S. NAVY
BROWNING, Captain Miles Rutherford, U.S. NAVY
HALSEY, Vice-Admiral William Frederick, Jr., U.S. NAVY
WALLIN, Captain Homer N., U.S. NAVY

REAR ADMIRAL WILSON BROWN, Jr., U.S. NAVY

"For exceptionally meritorious service to the Government of the United States in a duty of great responsibility as a Task Force Commander of the United States Pacific Fleet during a period at sea of approximately eight weeks in February and March, 1942, when he displayed the highest qualities of seamanship, leadership, endurance and tenacity while conducting extensive operations against, and a successful action with, enemy forces."

CAPTAIN MILES RUTHERFORD BROWNING, U.S. NAVY

Chief of Staff to a Task Force Commander, "In addition to contributing immeasurably to the success of our attack on Marshall and Gilbert Islands and raids on Wake and Marcus Islands..."

VICE-ADMIRAL WILLIAM FREDERICK HALSEY, Jr., U.S. NAVY

"For distinguished service in a duty of great responsibility. As Commanding Officer of the Marshall Islands raiding forces, U.S. Pacific Fleet, and especially for his brilliant and audacious attack against Marshall and Gilbert Islands, January 31, 1942. By his great skill and determination this drive inflicted great damage to enemy ships and planes."

CAPTAIN HOMER N. WALLIN, U.S. NAVY

"As Fleet Salvage Officer during the period following the attack on the United States Pacific Fleet in Pearl Harbor. Through his tireless and energetic devotion to duty, and benefitting by his past experiences, he accomplished the reclamation of damaged naval units expeditiously and with success beyond expectations."

Silver Star

SILVER STAR
ARMY AND NAVY

At the time of the Pearl Harbor attack, only Army personnel were eligible for the Silver Star. However, an Act of August 1942 authorized this award retroactively for the Navy. While the medals are identical and the qualifications almost similar, the formal wording differs.

The Army directive states, "The Silver Star is awarded to each person who, while an officer or enlisted man of the Army, is cited for gallantry in action in orders in which the Citation does not warrant the award of the Medal of Honor or the Distinguished Service Cross."

The Navy's requirements read, "Any person who, while serving in any capacity with the Navy of the United States since 6 December 1941, has distinguished himself conspicuously by gallantry and intrepidity in action, not sufficient to justify the award of the Medal of Honor or Navy Cross, also cases of persons previously submitted, recommended for Medal of Honor or Navy Cross or Distinguished Service Medal, and who were turned down, may be considered, all cases to be considered on records now in the Navy Department."

DESCRIPTION

The Silver Star has the appearance of a copper-zinc alloy with a small silver star in the center surrounded by a wreath enclosing radiations. The medal is suspended on a red, white and blue ribbon.

SILVER STARS for the NAVY

The following-named officers and enlisted men, United States Navy, were awarded a Silver Star by the Secretary of War for gallantry in action and participation in the accomplishment of an unusual and hazardous mission for the War Department in enemy controlled waters during January-March 1942, while members of the crew of the **USS TROUT**.

CHARLES JAMES BARR, Machinist's Mate First Class, USN
WILLIE GUY BENCH, Chief Electrician's Mate, USN
FRANK COLON BORAGO, Seaman Second Class, USN
ROBERT JOHN BROCKMAN, Torpedoman Second Class, USN

WILLIAM JOSEPH CASTENGERA, Torpedoman Second Class, USN
ALBERT HOBBS CLARK, Lieutenant, USN
DOMINICK CORBISIERE, Ship's Cook Second Class, USN
RAYMOND CONRAD JOSEPH COTE, Firecontrolman First Class, USN
JACK CECIL CRAIG, Torpedoman First Class, USN
FRANCIS JOSEPH DECKER, Machinist's Mate Second Class, USN
STEWART ALEXANDER DeHOSNERY, Mess Attendant First Class,
    USN
JOHN ALBERT DEVITT, Chief Electrician's Mate, USN
JAMES THOMAS DOWNS, Machinist's Mate Second Class, USN
STANLEY FESTIN, Seaman Second Class, USN
HAROLD ROY FISH, Seaman Second Class, USN
JENNINGS BRYAN FRAZER, Chief Machinist's Mate (AA), USN
WILLIAM HAROLD FRITSCH, Electrician's Mate Second Class, USN
GORDON INGVALD FROGNER, Apprentice Seaman, US NAVAL
    RESERVE
ALVIN LEROY GONYER, Signalman Third Class, USN
THEODORE LESTER GOODHUE, Torpedoman Second Class, USN
FREDERICK ALBERT GUNN, Lieutenant, USN
JOHN GEORGE GUTTERMUTH, Fireman Third Class, USN
JACOB HAGOPAN, Machinist's Mate First Class, USN
FREDERICK JOSEPH HARLFINGER II, Lieutenant, USN
DONALD WILLIAM HARRISON, Electrician's Mate Second Class, USN
RICHARD GATLING HAWN, Machinist's Mate Second Class, USN
JAMES ELTON JOY, Fireman Third Class, USN
ROBERT LUTHER HUGHES, Electrician's Mate Second Class, USN
WALTER ROBERT HUGHES, Jr., Apprentice Seaman, US NAVAL
    RESERVE
LONNIE DAVID JACKSON, Mess Attendant First Class, USN
ROBERT FRANKLIN JACKSON, Fireman Third Class, USN
THURMAN LOUIS JOINER, Torpedoman First Class, USN
KENNETH KARLYLE KAIL, Seaman First Class, USN
EDWIN ARNOLD KEIFER, Apprentice Seaman, USN
MORRIS HENRY KELTNER, Chief Quartermaster (AA), USN
HOMER LYMON KING, Torpedoman Second Class, USN
GLEN DIEVER KUMP, Seaman First Class, USN
ANTHONY LEON, Fireman Second Class, USN
ALBERT LEWIS LEIGHTLEY, Signalman First Class, USN
CLARE LIGGETT, Jr., Machinist's Mate Second Class, USN
JOHN WILLIAM MARSTERS, Chief Machinist's Mate (AA), USN

MAURICE LEONARD McCONNELL, Pharmacist's Mate First Class, USN
CHARLES H. McCOY, Apprentice Seaman, USN
ROBERT CARL MILLER, Seaman Second Class, USN
KENNETH EUGENE NEARMAN, Seaman First Class, USN
GEORGE THOMAS OWEN, Commander, USN
FELIX PERKOWSKY, Chief Torpedoman (PA), USN
RALPH RAYMOND PERRY, Machinist's Mate First Class, USN
FRED EUGENE PING, Seaman Second Class, USN
RAYMOND LESLIE PITTS, Ensign E-V (G), US NAVAL RESERVE
JOHN DANIEL REECE, Electrician's Mate First Class, USN
WILLIAM HENRY RICHARDSON, Radioman First Class, USN
HENRY LEE ROBERTS, Ship's Cook First Class, USN
FOREST GORDON ROBINSON, Chief Electrician's Mate, USN
JACOB ROSEN, Yeoman First Class, USN
CLIFFORD HARRISON SAUNDERS, Jr., Torpedoman First Class, USN
GEORGE H. SCHOTTLER, Ensign D-V(G), US NAVAL RESERVE
KENNETH IRWIN SCOTT, Seaman Second Class, USN
ROY JIM SCOTT, Jr., Seaman Second Class, V-3, US NAVAL RESERVE
JOHN FRANCIS SHIELDS, Gunner's Mate First Class, US NAVAL RESERVE
JESSE PHILLIP SOUTHERN, Chief Signalman (AA), USN
WILLIAM WILSON STANFORD, Machinist's Mate First Class, USN
VICTOR LaRUE TAYLOR, Radioman Third Class, USN
ROBERT MOODY THOMPSON, Apprentice Seaman, USN
EVERETT BRYANT WILLIS, Seaman Second Class, USN
HARRY EADES WOODWORTH, Lieutenant (jg), USN
HENRY JOSEPH ZARZECKI, Fireman Second Class, USN
CHESTER BARNARD ZEEMAN, Machinist's Mate Second Class, USN
ALBERT ZUBIK, Seaman Second Class, USN

CITATION for SILVER STAR for officers and enlisted men on above list:
"For gallantry in action and participation in the accomplishment of an unusual and hazardous mission for the War Department in enemy-controlled waters during January-March 1942, while members of the crew of the **USS TROUT.** Carrying a heavy load of antiaircraft ammunition urgently needed by the beleaguered forces of General Douglas MacArthur in the Philippine Islands, the **USS TROUT** departed from Pearl Harbor, T. H., for Corregidor Island, Manila Bay at 0900 12 January 1942, refueling at Midway Island on 16 January 1942. The **TROUT** proceeded on

the surface until 21 January, traveling submerged thereafter during daylight hours. At 0230, 27 January 1942, an unsuccessful night attack was made on a lighted enemy vessel, resulting in the **TROUT** being chased by the vessel at such a speed as to force the **TROUT** to dive in order to escape. On February 3, 1942, after dark, the **TROUT** made rendezvous off Corregidor with an escort motor torpedo boat. The **TROUT** then followed the escort at high speed through a winding passage in a mine field to South Dock, Corregidor Island, where she unloaded 3500 rounds of antiaircraft artillery ammunition for the Army Forces defending Bataan Peninsula and Corregidor. Twenty tons of gold and silver, securities, diplomatic and United States mail and two additional torpedoes were loaded on the **TROUT** for the return voyage. The **TROUT** cleared the Corregidor dock at 0300, 4 February and bottomed in Manila Bay during daylight 4 February. Surfacing that night, additional securities and mail were loaded before the **TROUT** departed from Manila Bay through the mine field. On the return trip one enemy merchant vessel and one patrol vessel were attacked and sunk. The **TROUT** arrived at Pearl Harbor 3 March 1942 after 51 days at sea."

IN ADDITION TO THE SILVER STAR RECIPIENTS OF THE USS TROUT, THE SILVER STAR WAS AWARDED TO THE FOLLOWING MEN OF THE U.S. NAVY AND U.S. MARINE CORPS:

*DAVIDSON, Second Lieutenant Carl R., U.S. MARINE CORPS RESERVES

KIEFER, Lieutenant (jg) Edwin H., U.S. NAVAL RESERVES

MARSHALL, Lieutenant Theodore W., U.S. NAVAL RESERVES

OWEN, Commodore George Thomas, U.S. NAVY

SHAPLEY, Major Alan, U.S. MARINE CORPS

VAN HOOSER, Seaman Second Class Joseph J., U.S. NAVY

WHITE, Lieutenant Commander David C., U.S. NAVY

Citations for the above five men are included in alphabetical order in the Citations listing of SILVER STARS for the ARMY.

* Posthumous award

SILVER STARS for the ARMY

The following Army personnel were awarded Silver Stars similar to those presented to Navy personnel:

ALBINO, Warrant Officer, Anthony A., Wheeler Field
*AVERY, Private First Class Robert L., Army Air Corps
BISHOP, First Lieutenant Samuel W., Army Air Corps
BLAKE, Lieutenant Colonel Gordon A., U.S. Army
*BROWN, Second Lieutenant Harry M., Army Air Corps
BURT, Sergeant William B., Army Air Corps
CARR, Sergeant Reuben A., Hickam Field
*CHAPMAN, Corporal Donald V., Army Air Corps
*DAINS, Second Lieutenant John L., Army Air Corps
*DAVIDSON, Second Lieutenant Carl R., U.S. Marine Corps Reserve
DRIER, Master Sergeant Elmer L., Army Air Corps
EHRKE, Sergeant Jack O., U.S. Army
FAY, Staff Sergeant Charles A., Army Air Corps
FINN, Corporal Edward, Army Air Corps
*FOX, Corporal Jack W., Army Air Corps
HAESSLY, Sergeant Robert J., Hickam
HALLOR, Captain Frederick C., Army Air Corps
HOWE, Staff Sergeant Sidney C., Hickam Field
HUNT, First Sergeant Wilbur K., Hickam Field
JESEK, Staff Sergeant Raymond F., Army Air Corps
KEISNER, Captain Donald M., U.S. Army
KIEFER, Lieutenant (jg) Edwin H., U.S. Naval Reserve
KLATZ, Staff Sergeant Lowell V., Coast Artillery, U.S. Army
LANDON, Major Truman H., Army Air Corps
MARSHALL, Lieutenant Theodore W., U.S. Naval Reserve
McBRIARITY, Private First Class Raymond, Army Air Corps
McNEILL, Sergeant Henry P. Jr., 31st Army Air Corps
*MEAGHER, Corporal Donald C., Army Air Corps
MEEHAN, Staff Sergeant John J., Army Air Corps
*MERITHEN, Private First Class William W., Army Air Corps
MIDDAUGH, Staff Sergeant Charles R., Army Air Corps
MISZCZUK, Private First Class Joseph P., Hickam Field
MOORE, First Lieutenant Malcolm A., Army Air Corps
MUCHA, Private First Class Paul, Hickam Field
NABORS, Technical Sergeant Bonnie V., Hickam Field

NEIS, Corporal Francis R., Army Air Corps
OWEN, Commander George Thomas, U.S. Navy
PETRAKOS, Sergeant Charles, Army Air Corps
PHILLIPS, Technical Sergeant Claude B., Army Air Corps
RASMUSSEN, Second Lieutenant Phillip M., Army Air Corps
ROGERS, First Lieutenant Robert J., Army Air Corps
SALTZMAN, Lieutenant Stephen G., U.S. Army
SANDERS, First Lieutenant Lewis M., Army Air Corps
SHAPLEY, Major Alan, U.S. Marine Corps
SHEFFIELD, Master Sergeant William K., Army Air Corps
*SMITH, Private Harry K., Army Air Corps
SMITH, Corporal Robert D., Army Air Corps
STODDAR, Second Lieutenant Loren A., Army Air Corps
THACKER, Second Lieutenant John M., Army Air Corps
TORTORA, Staff Sergeant Barnardina Q., Army Air Corps
VAN HOOSER, Seaman Second Class Joseph J., U.S. Navy
*VERNICK, Private First Class Edward F., Army Air Corps
WEBSTER, First Lieutenant John J., Army Air Corps
WHITE, Lieutenant Commander David C., U.S. Navy
*WHITEMAN, Second Lieutenant George A., Army Air Corps
YOUNG, Corporal Charles H., Army Air Corps

WARRANT OFFICER ANTHONY A. ALBINO, U.S. ARMY, HQ SQUADRON, 18th AIR BASE GROUP (R), Wheeler Field, Territory of Hawaii

"For gallantry in action. Mr. Albino, then a Technical Sergeant, Air Corps, during the Japanese air attack on the Island of Oahu, Territory of Hawaii, December 7, 1941, with disregard for his personal safety, volunteered to take the private automobile of an officer and secure additional ammunition for machine guns, which were set up on the rear porches of the Air Base Barracks. Permission to do this was granted and he twice drove to the Ordnance Warehouse at Wheeler Field, each trip requiring approximately one-quarter of an hour, and returned with sufficient boxes of ammunition to enable the machine gunners to continue the operation of their guns and to throw up a heavy curtain of fire. The area through which he drove was under exceptionally heavy fire from enemy planes. The action of Mr. Albino was an exceptionally meritorious one and was far beyond the normal call of duty, and his voluntary performance of this detail, his initiative, presence of mind, and coolness under fire reflect great credit upon himself and the military service."

*PRIVATE FIRST CLASS ROBERT L. AVERY, HQ AND HQ SQUADRON, 11th BOMBARDMENT GROUP (N), AIR CORPS, U.S. ARMY

"For gallantry in action during the Japanese aerial attack on Hickam Field, T.H. 7 December 1941. Private First Class Avery, for conspicuous bravery during the attack, assisted in putting a machine gun in action and later operated one of the guns. In the latter part of the attack Private First Class Avery was killed."

FIRST LIEUTENANT SAMUEL W. BISHOP, 44th PURSUIT SQUADRON, 18th PURSUIT GROUP, AIR CORPS, U.S. ARMY

"For gallantry in action at Bellows Field and over the Island of Oahu, T.H., and waters adjacent thereto, December 7, 1941. When surprised by a heavy air attack by Japanese Forces on Bellows Field and vicinity, and while under fire, he attempted to take off to engage the enemy, and in so doing was wounded and his plane so badly damaged that he was forced to make a crash landing in the waters nearby, and though wounded managed to swim ashore. Lt. Bishop's initiative, presence of mind, coolness under fire against overwhelming odds in his first battle, and determined action contributed to a large extent toward driving off this sudden enemy air attack."

LIEUTENANT COLONEL GORDON A. BLAKE, U.S. ARMY

"For gallantry in action at Hickam Field during the Japanese attack on the Island of Oahu, T.H. December 7, 1941. Lieutenant Colonel Blake remained in the Field control tower during the worst of the bombardment and calmly directed the safe landing of Flying Fortresses arriving from the Mainland."

*SECOND LIEUTENANT HARRY M. BROWN, 47th PURSUIT SQUADRON, 15th PURSUIT GROUP, AIR CORPS, U.S. ARMY

"For gallantry in action at Wheeler Field and over the Island of Oahu, T.H., and waters adjacent thereto, 7 December, 1941. When a surprise attack was launched by a large number of Japanese airplanes on Wheeler Field, T.H., and the vicinity thereto, Lt. Brown immediately proceeded by automobile to the Haleiwa Landing Field, a distance of approximately ten miles, where the planes of his squadron were located. The trip was made under heavy enemy fire. Upon arrival at Haleiwa Landing Field, he took off with an airplane for the purpose of attacking the enemy forces, without first obtaining information as to the number or type of planes in the attacking forces. He engaged an enemy aircraft and carried on combat until the enemy made his escape in a cloud formation. Shortly after this encounter, he flew over Kaene Point where two of the hostile forces pursued a friendly aircraft in battle. He immediately attacked, shooting one of the enemy down and aiding in driving off the other. Lt. Brown's expertness in battle during this engagement was instrumental in saving the life of the pilot in the friendly aircraft. Again, after being joined by another of the friendly forces, Lt. Brown attacked a hostile aircraft and continued to fire upon it until his ammunition ran out. The enemy aircraft was last seen by him heading out to sea in evident distress. Lt. Brown's initiative, presence of mind, coolness under fire, expert maneuvering of his plane, and determined action contributed to a large extent toward driving off the sudden and unexpected enemy air attack of 7 December 1941."

SERGEANT WILLIAM B. BURT, 86th OBSERVATION SQUADRON, ARMY AIR CORPS, U.S. ARMY

"For gallantry in action at Bellows Field, Territory of Hawaii, December 7, 1941. Private Burt, without prior training in the gunner's cockpit of an C-473 type observation airplane, sustained fire being delivered by diving flying enemy aircraft. His position was precarious due to the quality of enemy fire. However, Private Burt remained in his post until the conclusion of the raid."

SERGEANT REUBEN A. CARR, 22nd MATERIAL SQUADRON, HICKAM FIELD, U.S. ARMY

"For gallantry in action during the Japanese air attack on the Island of Oahu, T.H. December 7, 1941. With disregard for his personal safety, Carr volunteered to man a machine gun whose crew had been killed. Sergeant Carr then immediately set forth under continued fire to the dismantled gun, putting it in action, and continued to deliver an effective, accurate fire upon the Japanese aircraft throughout the entire raid. The bravery, coolness and good judgment displayed by Sergeant Carr on this occasion, reflect great credit upon himself and the military service."

*CORPORAL DONALD V. CHAPMAN, HQ AND HQ SQUADRON, 11th BOMBARDMENT GROUP (H), AIR CORPS, U.S. ARMY

"For gallantry in action during the Japanese aerial attack on Hickam Field, Territory of Hawaii, 7 December 1941. Corporal Chapman, conspicuous for his bravery under fire, assisted in repair of an airplane during the severe attack of bombing and strafing centered on the hangars. Corporal Chapman was killed in this attack."

*SECOND LIEUTENANT JOHN L. DAINS, 47th PURSUIT SQUADRON, 15th PURSUIT GROUP, AIR CORPS, U.S. ARMY

"For gallantry in action at Haleiwa Field and over the Island of Oahu, T.H., 7 December 1941. When the American forces on Oahu were surprised by a heavy attack launched by Japanese forces, Lt. Dains took off to combat the enemy in a F-40 type airplane with no advance information regarding the strength, disposition or type of enemy aircraft. Lt. Dains flew three missions on the morning of 7 December 1941, a total of approximately two and one-half hours. The first two missions were flown in a P-40 type airplane, and the third mission in a P-36 type airplane. He was killed in action during the third mission. Lt. Dains' undaunted courage and determined action, contributed to a large extent toward driving off the sudden enemy air attack."

*SECOND LIEUTENANT CARL R. DAVIDSON, U.S. MARINE CORPS RESERVE

"For extraordinary heroism as a pilot in Marine Fighter Squadron 211, in action against enemy Japanese forces during the defense of Wake Island, from 7 to 22 December 1941. Skilled as an airman, gallant as an officer and determined and aggresive in whatever he was assigned or voluntarily undertook to do throughout the bitter days of combat with a vastly superior enemy force, Second Lieutenant Davidson assumed a major role in maintaining morale among officers and men imperiled with him, sustaining their spirits by his own unwavering high courage and inspiring them to greater effort by his heroic work in rescuing wounded from burning airplanes and camp areas and in reorganizing the unit following the first devastating enemy raid. Carrying out his daily tasks and his part in combat operations with initiative and fortitude during this prolonged period of siege, 2nd Lt. Davidson went up to fight two full squadrons of Japanese aircraft on 22 December, and with only one other Marine plane for assistance, pressed home a vigorous attack against the large hostile force, diverting many enemy planes from the raid on Wake before he was shot down at sea following a fearless engagement with six Japanese fighter craft. His brilliant leadership and unswerving devotion to duty in the face of almost certain death constantly inspired the stouthearted defenders of this tiny island, and his valiant conduct throughout reflects the highest credit upon 2nd Lt. Davidson and the U.S. Naval Service. He gallantly gave his life for his country."

MASTER SERGEANT ELMER L. DRIER, 23rd BOMBARDMENT SQUADRON, 5th BOMBARDMENT GROUP (H), AIR CORPS, U.S. ARMY

"For gallantry in action during the Japanese aerial attack on Hickam Field, Territory of Hawaii, 7 December 1941. Master Sergeant Drier, conspicuous for bravery, was present at the hangar throughout the entire raid, assisting in salvage of aiplane parts. Sergeant Drier's actions during the attack helped to save large numbers of planes from destruction by fire."

SERGEANT JACK O. EHRKE, HQ HAWAIIAN DEPARTMENT, U.S. ARMY

"For heroism in action during the attack on Hickam Field by Japanese forces (aircraft) on December 7, 1941. Sergeant Ehrke, on duty as Supply Sergeant, although severely wounded by flying shrapnel from aerial bombs during the early part of the attack, continued to perform his duty as Supply Sergeant and succeeded in distributing many pieces of necessary paraphernalia, such as steel helmets, rifles, ammunition, etc. After diligently performing his duties in the supply section, he then continued to rescue and evacuate wounded men from the attacked area. Only after his duty had been well performed did he report to the hospital for treatment. Sergeant Ehrke displayed a devotion to duty and a spirit of self sacrifice which was an inspiration to the entire command. The heroism displayed by Sergeant Ehrke on this occasion reflected great credit upon himself and the military service."

STAFF SERGEANT CHARLES A. FAY, 72nd PURSUIT SQUADRON, 15th PURSUIT GROUP, AIR CORPS, U.S. ARMY

"For gallantry in action at Wheeler Field, Island of Oahu, T.H., 7 December 1941, When surprised by a heavy air attack by Japanese forces on Wheeler Field and vicinity at approximately 8 a.m., he, with utter disregard of his personal safety proceeded to the hangar line and taxied aircraft out of the burning hangars. He was under constant enemy fire, and though twice hit by machine gun bullets, he continued with his task until completed. His initiative, presence of mind, coolness under fire, and determined action contributed to a large extent toward driving off this sudden, unexpected enemy air attack. The heroism displayed by Staff Sergeant Fay on this occasion reflects great credit upon himself and the military service."

CORPORAL EDWARD FINN, 42nd BOMBARDMENT SQUADRON (H), 11th BOMBARDMENT GROUP (H) AIR CORPS, U.S. ARMY

"For gallantry in action during Japanese aerial attack on Hickam Field, T.H., 7 December 1941. Corporal Finn, having no previous instruction in the mechanism of machine guns, secured and mounted a .50 caliber machine gun, and delivered effective fire upon the enemy."

*CORPORAL JACK W. FOX, 31st BOMBARDMENT SQUADRON (H), 5th BOMBARDMENT GROUP (H), AIR CORPS, U.S. ARMY

"For gallantry in action in the Japanese aerial attack on Hickam Field, T.H., 7 December 1941. Corporal Fox, conspicuous for his bravery and coolness, caused the lives of a large group of men to be saved by ordering the men from unprotected areas to the shelter of the barracks, only a few seconds before the area was bombed and strafed by enemy aircraft. During the second attack, Corporal Fox, seeing a machine gun jam, started to the aid of the crew to reduce the jam. At this time a heavy attack of strafing and bombing centered on this area. A fragmentation bomb exploded near Corporal Fox; he was killed instantly."

SERGEANT ROBERT J. HAESSLY, 22nd MATERIAL SQUADRON, HICKAM FIELD, TERRITORY OF HAWAII

"For gallantry in action during the Japanese air attack on the Island of Oahu, T.H., 7 December 1941. With disregard for his personal safety, Sgt. Haessly volunteered to man a .50 caliber machine gun whose crew had been killed and the gun itself damaged. Sgt. Haessly succeeded in putting the gun back in action and continued to operate the gun against enemy aircraft. The bravery, coolness and good judgment displayed by Sergeant Haessly on this occasion reflects great credit upon himself and the military service."

CAPTAIN FREDERICK C. HALLOR, AIR CORPS, HICKAM FIELD, T.H.

"For heroism in action during the attack on Hickam Field by Japanese forces (aircraft) on December 7, 1941. Captain Hallor, in addition to being Commanding Officer of the 22nd Material Squadron Air Corps, assumed command of the 23rd Material Squadron, Air Corps, in the absence of its Commanding Officer. Captain Hallor displayed marked heroism in coordinating the activities of these two squadrons so that a maximum of fire power was gained, and casualties were held to a minimum. Captain Hallor acted with complete disregard for his own personal safety while under fire throughout the attack. In addition, Captain Hallor gave valuable assistance to an Aviation Cadet who had been wounded in obtaining medical attention. Captain Hallor showed unusual courage and bravery throughout the entire bombardment and proved himself a capable Commander in every respect. The heroism displayed by Captain Hallor on this occasion reflected great credit upon himself and the military service."

STAFF SERGEANT SIDNEY C. HOWE, 19TH TRANSPORT SQUADRON, HICKAM FIELD, T.H.

"For heroism in action during the attack on Hickam Field by Japanese forces (aircraft) on December 7, 1941. Technical Sergeant Howe, with utter disregard for his personal safety, in the face of overwhelming enemy aerial machine gunnery and aerial bombardment, returned the enemy fire with heroism until severely wounded by fragments of an exploding bomb, resulting in the loss of his left arm. The heroism displayed by Technical Sergeant Howe reflected great credit upon himself and the military service."

FIRST SERGEANT WILBUR K. HUNT, 22nd MATERIAL SQUADRON, HICKAM FIELD, T.H.

"For heroism in action during the attack on Hickam Field, T.H., by Japanese Forces (aircraft) on December 7, 1941. Technical Sergeant Hunt performed exceptionally meritorious service and displayed outstanding bravery in assisting the Squadron Commander of the 22nd Material Squadron in dispersing the squadron under fire and bombardment to positions of vantage to deliver return fire and to secure adequate cover and safety, thus contributing in reducing the number of battle casualties. The heroism displayed by Technical Sergeant Hunt on this occasion reflected great credit upon himself and the military service."

STAFF SERGEANT RAYMOND F. JESEK, 7th BOMBER COMMAND, ARMY AIR CORPS, U.S. ARMY

"For gallantry during the December 7, 1941 attack on Hickam Field, T.H., Sergeant Jesek, though already wounded, proceeded to drive an ambulance through the strafing and bombing, picking up wounded and taking them to the hospital."

CAPTAIN DONALD M. KEISNER, U.S. ARMY

"For gallantry during the December 7, 1941 attack."

LIEUTENANT (jg) EDWIN H. KIEFER, U.S. NAVAL RESERVE

"Helped maintain by hand ammunition supply to antiaircraft guns until he was overcome by smoke and fire."

STAFF SERGEANT LOWELL V. KLATZ, COAST ARTILLERY REGIMENT, U.S. ARMY

"When on duty near Wahiawa, Staff Sergeant Lowell V. Klatz distinguished himself with gallantry in action for bringing down a Japanese plane with his automatic rifle. He voluntarily and on his own initiative without regard for his own safety left the shelter of the Command Post in the face of heavy fire from enemy planes. He coolly waited in an exposed position until one of the enemy planes approached within 100 yards and then deliberately aimed automatic rifle fire at one of the two enemy planes. Firing along with Second Lieutenant Stephen G. Saltzman, the combined fire caused the enemy plane to crash resulting in the destruction of the airship and its crew. The cool determination and disregard for his personal safety displayed was an inspiration to the members of his regiment."

MAJOR TRUMAN H. LANDON, 18th RECONNAISSANCE SQUADRON (H), ARMY AIR CORPS, U.S., ARMY

"For gallantry in action, conspicuous bravery, coolness and expert handling of his airplane during the Japanese aerial attack on Hickam Field, T.H., 7 December 1941. Major Landon, Echelon Commander on a flight from Hamilton Field, California, after an all night flight and with only a small quantity of gasoline remaining which necessitated an early landing, arrived in the vicinity of Hickam Field during the Japanese attack and was subjected to heavy anti-aircraft fire and was attacked by Japanese aircraft. Major Landon's flight was unarmed and unprepared for an attack and rather than risk damaging the aircraft under his control by landing in an inadequate, although protected field, brought about the safe landing of his flight through his skill, coolness and daring under fire."

LIEUTENANT THEODORE W. MARSHALL, U.S. NAVAL RESERVES

"Serving with Patrol Squadron 21, during the Japanese attack on Pearl Harbor, T.H., December 7, 1941, he commandeered a truck and ferried personnel to battle stations. Later, pursued by a torpedo bomber, he attacked enemy craft for 150 miles." (sic)

PRIVATE FIRST CLASS RAYMOND McBRIARITY, 86th OBSERVATION SQUADRON, AIR CORPS, U.S. ARMY

"For gallantry in action at Bellows Field, Territory of Hawaii, 7 December 1941. Private First Class McBriarity proceeded under fire to obtain and mount in his assigned airplane a machine gun which he then manned to deliver fire against the enemy. With complete disregard for his personal safety and during overwhelming machine gun fire of the enemy, he remained at his station until the conclusion of the raid."

SERGEANT HENRY P. McNEILL, JR., 31st BOMBARDMENT SQUADRON (H), 5th BOMBARDMENT GROUP (H) ARMY AIR CORPS, U.S. ARMY

"For gallantry in action during the Japanese aerial attack on Hickam Field, Territory of Hawaii, 7 December 1941. Sergeant McNeill organized a fire fighting crew during the strafing and succeeded in extinguishing fires on two planes and saving valuable equipment of the third. He then took a tug and towed the two planes to dispersed positions. Again he was subjected to extremely heavy strafing."

*CORPORAL DONALD C. MEAGHER, ARMY AIR CORPS

NOTE: No specifics are available as to Corporal Meagher's duty station on 7 December 1941. His formal Citation was not included with other groups but the following information was culled from a Berkeley, California news clipping of June 1984.

"Corporal Meagher dispersed one of the attacking Japanese planes with the front guns of a grounded American craft. He was killed when his plane was struck by an exploding shell."

STAFF SERGEANT JOHN J. MEEHAN, 4th RECONNAISSANCE SQUADRON (H), 5th BOMBARDMENT GROUP (H), ARMY AIR CORPS, U.S. ARMY.

"For gallantry in action in the Japanese aerial attack on Hickam Field, Territory of Hawaii, 7 December 1941. Sergeant Meehan was wounded during the attack but refused to disclose he was wounded until after he had dispersed the planes, which at the time of the attack were in hangars, subjected to strafing and bombing."

*PRIVATE FIRST CLASS WILLIAM W. MERITHEN, HQ AND HQ SQUADRON, 11th BOMBARDMENT GROUP (H), AIR CORPS, U.S. ARMY

"For gallantry in action during Japanese aerial attack on Hickam Field, Territory of Hawaii, 7 December 1941. Private First Class Merithen, conspicuous for his bravery, assisted in the repair of airplanes during a severe attack of bombing and strafing centered on the hangars. Private Merithen was killed in this attack."

STAFF SERGEANT CHARLES R. MIDDAUGH, 18th AIR BASE SQUADRON, HICKAM FIELD, T.H., AIR CORPS, U.S. ARMY

"For heroism in action during the attack on Hickam Field by Japanese Forces (aircraft) on December 7, 1941. Staff Sergeant Middaugh was a gunner on a .30 Caliber machine gun during the second raid on Hickam Field. As a Japanese plane headed straight for his gun position, Staff Sergeant Middaugh took the plane under fire. Staff Sergeant Middaugh knew he was making direct hits through the use of tracer bullets. Smoke trailed from the plane which banked over Pearl Harbor and flew toward Barbers Point, appearing to be out of control. The heroism, devotion to duty and spirit of self-sacrifice displayed by Staff Sergeant Middaugh on this occasion reflected great credit upon himself and the military service."

PRIVATE FIRST CLASS JOSEPH P. MISZCZUK, 12th SIGNAL PLATOON (AB) HICKAM FIELD, T.H., U.S. ARMY

"For gallantry in action during the Japanese air attack on the Island of Oahu, Territory of Hawaii, December 7, 1941. With disregard for his personal safety, he advanced under fire to a position in the parking lot located between Scott Circle and Atterbury Circle, a distance of approximately 50 yards, where two men had stopped, exhausted, while carrying a wounded man to the Station Hospital. Private First Class Miszczuk then helped the exhausted soldiers to cover of foliage where the men were concealed from view of the enemy and then carried the wounded soldier to the hospital, being under steady fire by enemy machine gunners. The bravery, coolness and good judgment displayed by Private First Class Miszczuk on this occasion, reflect great credit upon himself and the military service."

FIRST LIEUTENANT MALCOLM A. MOORE, 46th PURSUIT SQUADRON, 15th PURSUIT GROUP, AIR CORPS, U.S. ARMY
"For gallantry in action at Wheeler Field and over the island of Oahu, T.H., and waters adjacent thereto, 7 December 1941. When surprised by a heavy air attack by Japanese forces on Wheeler Field and vicinity at approximately 8 a.m. he proceeded by automobile, under fire, to the hangar line where he assisted in extinguishing a fire in the hangar, thereby saving aircraft and ammunition. While the aircraft was being loaded with ammunition he was continuously under enemy fire of both cannon and machineguns. As soon as his guns were loaded he immediately took off for the purpose of attacking the invading forces, without first obtaining information as to the number or type of Japanese in the attacking force, and proceeded to a position over Kaena Point where he encountered an enemy aircraft which he immediately attacked and made a number of direct hits. Due to a heavy cloud formation the enemy aircraft managed to make his escape. Unable to locate any other enemy craft he returned to Wheeler Field. Lt. Moore's initiative, presence of mind, coolness under fire, expert maneuvering of his plane, and determined action contributed to a large extent toward driving off this sudden, unexpected enemy air attack."

PRIVATE FIRST CLASS PAUL MUCHA, 12th SIGNAL PLATOON (AB), HICKAM FIELD, T.H., U.S. ARMY
"For gallantry in action during the Japanese air attack on the Island of Oahu, Territory of Hawaii, December 7, 1941. With disregard for his personal safety, Private First Class Mucha advanced under fire to a position in the parking lot located between Scott Circle and Atterbury Circle, a distance of approximately 50 yards, where two men had stopped, exhausted, while carrying a wounded man to the Station Hospital. Private First Class Mucha then helped the exhausted soldiers to a cover of foliage where the men were concealed from view of the enemy and then carried the wounded soldier to the hospital, being under steady fire by enemy machine gunners. The bravery, coolness and good judgment displayed by Private First Class Mucha on this occasion, reflect great credit upon himself and the military service."

TECHNICAL SERGEANT BONNIE V. NABORS, 19th TRANSPORT SQUADRON, HICKAM FIELD, T.H., U.S. ARMY
"For heroism in action during the attack on Hickam Field by Japanese Forces (aircraft) on December 7, 1941. Sergeant Nabors proceeded to

hangar No. 17 where the squadron's planes were parked. The adjacent hangar, No. 15, had already been severely bombed. A plane close by had been hit and was burning rapidly and its proximity to the transport planes greatly endangered them. Noting this danger, Sergeant Nabors assisted the crew of one of the planes in rolling it back from the hangar a short distance. Although under fire by the enemy, Sergeant Nabors climbed into the plane, opened the escape hatch, and from this position assisted the pilot in taxiing the plane through debris and dense smoke to a position of comparative safety. Sergeant Nabors displayed quick thinking, bravery, coolness and a great devotion to duty by his action and was an inspiration to those who observed these acts. The heroism displayed by Sergeant Nabors on this occasion reflected great credit upon himself and the military service."

CORPORAL FRANCIS R. NEIS, 31st BOMBARDMENT SQUADRON (H), 5th BOMBARDMENT GROUP (H), ARMY AIR CORPS, U.S. ARMY

"For gallantry in action in the Japanese aerial attack on Hickam Field, T.H., 7 December 1941. Corporal Neis, conspicuous for his bravery, with disregard for his own safety during the strafing by Japanese planes went to the aid of a wounded soldier some distance from the hangar and while returning the wounded man to the hangar was strafed by machine gun fire. Corporal Neis was hurt in the strafing, the wounded man was killed. Corporal Neis returned to the field to aid another wounded man. He was again subjected to strafing but brought this man to safety in the hangar."

COMMANDER GEORGE THOMAS OWEN, U.S. NAVY

"As acting Commanding Officer of the **USS CURTIS,** he organized his command in a spirited and effective defense."

SERGEANT CHARLES PETRAKOS, 4th RECONNAISSANCE SQUADRON (N), 5th BOMBARDMENT GROUP (H) ARMY AIR CORPS

"For gallantry in action in the Japanese aerial attack on Hickam Field, T.H., 7 December 1941. Sergeant Petrakos was in the plane loading bombs when the attack started. He immediately volunteered his services as gunner and manned one of the guns on the plane. During the attack Sergeant Petrakos shot down one Japanese plane and disabled another."

TECHNICAL SERGEANT CLAUDE B. PHILLIPS, 4th RECON-
NAISSANCE, SQUADRON (H), 5th BOMBARDMENT GROUP,
(H), ARMY AIR CORPS

"For gallantry in action during Japanese aerial attack on Hickam Field,
T.H., 7 December 1941. Sergeant Phillips was helping load bombs in the
plane when the bombing and strafing started. He immediately manned
one of the machine guns in the plane and returned effective fire on the
enemy aircraft. During the second raid Sergeant Phillips shot down one
plane and disabled another."

SECOND LIEUTENANT PHILIP M. RASMUSSEN, 46th PURSUIT
SQUADRON, 15th PURSUIT GROUP, AIR CORPS, U.S. ARMY

"For gallantry in action at Wheeler Field and over the Island of Oahu,
T.H. and waters adjacent thereto, December 7, 1941. When surprised by
a heavy air attack by Japanese forces on Wheeler Field and vicinity he
took off for the purpose of attacking the invading forces, without first obtaining information as to the number or type of Japanese in the attacking
force, and proceeded to patrol in the vicinity of Bellows Field, where he
encountered six enemy aircraft. Though outnumbered with only three
other aircraft in the flight he immediately attacked the enemy formation
and shot one down in flames. He returned his plane safely to Wheeler
Field although it had been damaged by enemy machine gun and cannon
fire during the encounter. Lt. Rasmussen's presence of mind, coolness
under fire against overwhelming odds in his first battle, expert maneuvering of his plane, and determined action contributed to a large extent
toward driving off this sudden enemy air attack."

FIRST LIEUTENANT ROBERT J. ROGERS, 47th PURSUIT SQUAD-
RON, 15th PURSUIT GROUP, AIR CORPS, U.S. ARMY

"For gallantry in action over the island of Oahu, T.H. and waters adjacent thereto, December 7, 1941. When surprised by a heavy air attack
by Japanese forces on Wheeler Field and vicinity at approximately 8 a.m.,
he proceeded by automobile to Haleiwa Landing Field, a distance of approximately ten miles, where the planes of his squadron were stationed.
As soon as his plane had been serviced he immediately took off for the
purpose of attacking the invading forces, without first obtaining
information as to the number or type of Japanese in the attacking force,
and proceeded to patrol in the vicinity of Haleiwa, where he encountered
an enemy aircraft which he immediately attacked, and when last seen by
him it was disappearing into a cloud bank streaming black smoke. After

this encounter, he and one other pursuit ship attacked two enemy aircraft in the vicinity of Kaena Point. While engaged in this combat his plane was hit by enemy fire. After this encounter he returned to Haleiwa and landed. Lieutenant Rogers' initiative, presence of mind, and coolness under fire and expert maneuvering of his plane, and determined action contributed to a large extent toward driving off this sudden, unexpected enemy air attack."

LIEUTENANT STEPHEN G. SALTZMAN, U.S. ARMY

"For gallantry in action at Wahiawa, Lieutenant Stephen G. Saltzman brought down a Japanese plane with his automatic rifle. Along with Staff Sergeant Lowell V. Klatz, he voluntarily and on his own initiative without regard for his own safety left the shelter of the Command Post in the face of heavy fire from enemy planes. He coolly waited in an exposed position until one of the enemy planes approached within 100 yards, and then delivered armed automatic rifle fire at one of the two enemy planes. His fire, combined with that of Klatz, caused the plane to crash, resulting in the destruction of ship and crew. The cool determination and disregard for his personal safety displayed was an inspiration to members of his regiment."

FIRST LIEUTENANT LEWIS M. SANDERS, 46th PURSUIT SQUADRON, 15th PURSUIT GROUP, AIR CORPS, UNITED STATES ARMY

"For gallantry in action at Wheeler Field and over the island of Oahu, T.H. and waters adjacent thereto, 7 December 1941. During the surprise attack by Japanese forces on 7 December 1941, Lieutenant Sanders took off with one flight for the purpose of attacking the invading forces, without first securing information as to the number or type of attacking Japanese aircraft. He proceeded to patrol the vicinity of Bellows Field, where he engaged six enemy planes. Although greatly outnumbered he succeeded in shooting down one enemy aircraft. Lt. Sanders' initiative, presence of mind, coolness under fire, and expert maneuvering of his plane, contributed to a large extent toward driving off this sudden, unexpected enemy air attack."

MAJOR ALAN SHAPLEY, U.S. MARINE CORPS

"For gallant and courageous conduct during the attack on the United States Pacific Fleet by enemy Japanese forces in Pearl Harbor, T.H.,

December 7, 1941. While swimming toward Ford Island after his ship had been bombed and set afire by the enemy, Major Shapley noticed a ship-mate in distress in the water and about to go under. With no thought for his own safety, he braved the hazards of continuous enemy strafing and bombing to swim to the assistance of his helpless shipmate and, although exhausted himself, persisted in his efforts until he finally succeeded in bringing him safely ashore. His heroic action, performed at great peril to his own life, was in keeping with the highest traditions of the United States Naval Service."

MASTER SERGEANT WILLIAM E. SHEFFIELD, 234th BOM-BARDMENT SQUADRON, 5th BOMBARDMENT GROUP (R), ARMY AIR CORPS

"For gallantry in action during the Japanese aerial attack on Hickam Field, Territory of Hawaii, 7 December 1941. Master Sergeant Sheffield was conspicuous for his actions in the efforts to save several airplanes from destruction by fire."

*PRIVATE HARRY K. SMITH, HQ & HQ SQUADRON, 11th BOM-BARDMENT GROUP (H), ARMY AIR CORPS

"For gallantry in action during Japanese aerial attack on Hickam Field, T.H., 7 December 1941. Private Smith, conspicuous for bravery and courage, assisted in the repair of airplanes during the severe attacks of bombing and strafing centered on the hangars. Private Smith was killed in this attack."

CORPORAL ROBERT D. SMITH, 31st BOMBARDMENT SQUAD-RON (H) 5th BOMBARDMENT GROUP (R), AIR CORPS, U.S. ARMY

"For gallantry in action during Japanese aerial attack on Hickam Field, Territory of Hawaii, 7 December 1941. Corporal Smith assisted in ex-tinguishing two planes set afire by strafing and bombing, and saving valuable equipment from the third. After extinguishing the fires, Cor-poral Smith assisted in towing two airplanes to dispersed positions under extreme heavy strafing and bombing."

SECOND LIEUTENANT LOREN A. STODDARD, AIR CORPS, HICKAM FIELD, T.H., U.S. ARMY

"For heroism in action during the attack on Hickam Field by Japanese Forces (aircraft) on December 7, 1941. Lieutenant Stoddard, a pilot in the 19th Transport Squadron, proceeded to hangar No. 17 where the squadron's planes were parked. The adjacent hangar, No. 15, had already been severely bombed. A plane close by had been hit and was burning rapidly and its proximity to the transport planes greatly endangered them. Noting this danger Lieutenant Stoddard, on his own initiative and without orders, started the motors of one of the planes after the crew had rolled it back from the hangar a short distance. Although under fire by the enemy, Lieutenant Stoddard, with a crew member observing for him through the escape hatch, taxied the plane through debris and smoke to a relatively safe position on the field away from the hangars. Lieutenant Stoddard displayed fast thinking, bravery, coolness and a great devotion to duty by his action and was an inspiration to all who saw him. The heroism displayed by Lieutenant Stoddard on this occasion reflected great credit upon himself and the military service.

SECOND LIEUTENANT JOHN M. THACKER, 46th PURSUIT SQUADRON, 15th PURSUIT GROUP, ARMY AIR CORPS, U.S. ARMY

"For gallantry in action over the island of Oahu, T.H., and waters adjacent thereto, December 7, 1941. When surprised by a heavy air attack by Japanese forces on Wheeler Field and vicinity at approximately 8 a.m., he proceeded by automobile to the hangar line where he joined a flight of pursuit aircraft which took off from Wheeler Field for the purpose of attacking the invading forces, without first obtaining information as to the number or type of Japanese in the attacking forces. The flight encountered an enemy formation of six aircraft in the vicinity of Bellows Field, and though the enemy force was numerically superior, Lt. Thacker and other members of the flight immediately attacked the enemy formation. He remained in the attack until after his guns became jammed. Lt. Thacker returned his plane safely to Wheeler Field although it had been hit by cannon fire during the encounter. Lt. Thacker's initiative, presence of mind, coolness under fire against overwhelming odds in his first battle, expert maneuvering of his plane, and determined action contributed to a large extent toward driving off this sudden enemy air attack."

STAFF SERGEANT BARNARDINA Q. TORTORA, 23rd BOM-
BARDMENT SQUADRON (H), 5th BOMBARDMENT GROUP (H),
ARMY AIR CORPS, U.S. ARMY

"For gallantry in action in the Japanese aerial attack on Hickam Field,
T.H., 7 December 1941. Sergeant Tortora, conspicuous for his bravery, taxied a B-18 across the runway while under heavy enemy bombing and aircraft fire to a safe dispersed position."

SEAMAN SECOND CLASS JOSEPH J. VAN HOOSER, U.S. NAVY

"For meritorious conduct at the peril of his own life during the attack
on the U.S. Pacific Fleet in Pearl Harbor, Territory of Hawaii by Japanese
forces on December 7, 1941. After having saved his own life by swimming
from the capsized **USS UTAH** to the shore of Ford Island he heard cries
of distress from his shipmates in the water. In spite of enemy strafing and
bombing and while in full uniform, he immediately swam back towards
the ship and succeeded in rescuing Harold H. Ray, Sea2c, USN, bringing
him to the shore. Immediately thereafter he made at least four more trips
to the ship's side, assisting a shipmate in distress each time. His initiative,
courage, presence of mind and unselfishness were in keeping with the
best traditions of the naval service."

*PRIVATE FIRST CLASS EDWARD F. VERNICK, HQ & HQ
SQUADRON, 11th BOMBARDMENT GROUP (H), AIR CORPS, U.S.
ARMY

"For gallantry in action during Japanese aerial attack on Hickam Field,
Territory of Hawaii, 7 December 1941. Private First Class Vernick, conspicuous for his bravery, assisted in repairing an airplane during the
severe attack of bombing and strafing of the hangars. Private First Class
Vernick was killed in this attack."

FIRST LIEUTENANT JOHN J. WEBSTER, 47th PURSUIT SQUAD-
RON, 15th PURSUIT GROUP, AIR CORPS, U.S. ARMY

"For gallantry in action at Wheeler Field and over the island of Oahu,
T.H. and waters adjacent thereto, December 7, 1941. When surprised by
a heavy air attack by Japanese forces on Wheeler Field and vicinity approximately 9 a.m. he obtained a Gerand rifle and ammunition and kept
up a continuous fire until all enemy aircraft had disappeared. He then
proceeded by automobile to Haleiwa Landing Field, a distance of approximately ten miles, where the planes of his squadron were stationed. He
took off for the purpose of attacking the invading forces, without first ob-

taining information as to the number or type of Japanese in the attacking forces, and proceeded to patrol in the vicinity of Haleiwa, then toward Kaena Point, where he encountered two enemy aircraft. Though outnumbered he immediately attacked the enemy formation and continued to engage them until after his controls were damaged and he had received a leg wound from enemy machine gun fire. He then returned his plane safely to the field. Lt. Webster's initiative, presence of mind, coolness under fire against overwhelming odds in his first battle, expert maneuvering of his plane, and determined action contributed to a large extent toward driving off this sudden, unexpected enemy air attack."

LIEUTENANT COMMANDER DAVID C. WHITE, U.S. NAVY

"For conspicuous gallantry and intrepidity in action as Commanding Officer of the **USS PLUNGER** during a successful and aggressive submarine patrol in enemy Japanese controlled waters. Skillfully and courageously pressing home his attacks against the enemy, Lieutenant Commander White enabled his ship to sink one enemy destroyer of 1,315 tons and to damage another of approximately the same size. Despite enemy counter efforts, he dauntlessly brought the **PLUNGER** through without damage and his crew home without loss or injury. His expert seamanship and heroic devotion to duty were in keeping with the highest traditions of the United States Naval Service."

*SECOND LIEUTENANT GEORGE A. WHITEMAN, 44th PURSUIT SQUADRON, 18th PURSUIT GROUP, AIR CORPS, U.S. ARMY

"For gallantry in action at Bellows Field, island of Oahu, T.H., December 7, 1941. When surprised by a heavy air attack by Japanese forces on Bellows Field and vicinity and while under fire, he attempted to take off to engage the enemy, and while so doing was shot down in flames by enemy aircraft."

CORPORAL CHARLES H. YOUNG, 42nd BOMBARDMENT SQUADRON (H) 11th BOMBARDMENT GROUP (H), AIR CORPS, U.S. ARMY

"For gallantry in action during Japanese aerial attack on Hickam Field, Territory of Hawaii, 7 December 1941. Sergeant Phillips was helping load bombs in the plane when the bombing and strafing started. He immediately manned one of the machine guns in the plane and returned effective fire on the enemy aircraft. During the second raid Sergeant Phillips shot down one plane and disabled another."

Legion of Merit

LEGION OF MERIT

The Legion of Merit is awarded to personnel of the armed forces of the United States and the Philippines, and personnel of the armed forces of friendly foreign nations who, since 8 September 1939, shall have distinguished themselves by exceptionally meritorious conduct in the performance of outstanding services.

Unlike other medals, there are four degrees of the Legion of Merit, but, only when awarded to personnel of an armed force of a friendly foreign nation. These degrees are Chief Commander, Commander, Officer and Legionnaire. Members of U.S. Armed Forces receive this award without reference to degree.

DESCRIPTION

This colorful medal of red, white and green enamel is two inches in diameter, the largest of all combat medals. Some collectors claim it bears a small amount of gold. In the center, thirteen tiny white stars on a field of blue emerge from a circle of clouds. Backing the stars is a laurel wreath circled by five sets of crossed war arrows. The medal then radiates outward into a heraldic cross.

The reverse bears the wordings, "United States of America," and a Latin motto, which, translated means, "God has favored our undertaking." Space is allowed for the engraving of the recipient's name.

Only four Legion of Merit medals were awarded for outstanding service during the early days of the war. Those so honored were:

FURLONG, Rear Admiral William Rea, U.S. Navy
LEWIS, Rear Admiral Spencer S., U.S. Navy
STEELE, Captain James M., U.S. Navy
THOMAS, Captain Robert Ellsworth, U.S. Navy
WHITAKER, Captain Francis H., U.S. Navy

CITATIONS FOR LEGION OF MERIT

REAR ADMIRAL WILLIAM REA FURLONG, U.S. NAVY

Acting Commandant and later as Commandant of the Navy Yard at Pearl Harbor. "By his splendid initiative, sound judgment and untiring efforts in directing the difficult salvage activities, he was largely responsible for the successful and expeditious manner in which the vital operations were completed."

NOTE: Rear Admiral Furlong, ComMinePac was on his flag ship **USS OGLALA,** 7 December, with the SOPA (Senior Officer Present Afloat) duty. He issued the "All ships sortie." order (Depart from port.) on December 7th.

REAR ADMIRAL SPENCER S. LEWIS, U.S. NAVY

Chief of Staff and aide to Task Force Commander in Pacific Area for first ten months of WW II.

Citation not available.

CAPTAIN JAMES M. STEELE, U.S. NAVY

Salvage Superintendent following Japanese action at Pearl Harbor. "He skillfully organized personnel and expedited the procurement of material and equipment necessary to the accomplishment of the important tasks assigned him."

NOTE: Capt. Steele was Commanding Officer of the **USS UTAH** which was bombed and capsized during the Japanese attack on the fleet 7 December. The radio controlled target ship **UTAH** was not salvageable.

CAPTAIN ROBERT ELLSWORTH THOMAS, CEC, U.S. NAVY

"The outstanding accomplishments in Navy base construction in the Pacific Area during 1942 were largely due to Captain Thomas' professional ability, keen foresight and perseverance in the face of almost insurmountable difficulties."

CAPTAIN FRANCIS H. WHITAKER, U.S. NAVY

Member of the Planning Division and later as Hull Superintendent and Salvage Superintendent following raid on Pearl Harbor 7 December 1941.

Distinguished Flying Cross

DISTINGUISHED FLYING CROSS

All members of the Army, Navy, Marine Corps, Coast Guard, National Guard and several Reserve Corps were eligible for the Distinguished Flying Cross on 7 December 1941. The individual must have distinguished himself by heroism or extraordinary achievement while participating in aerial flight.

DESCRIPTION

The medal is made of bronze. On the obverse is a four-bladed propeller superimposed on a maltese cross. The cross is superimposed on a bronze square with corrugations radiating from the center. The reverse is blank. The medal is suspended from a ribbon with narrow red center, flanked by white and blue stripes of varied widths.

The Distinguished Flying Cross was awarded to combatants of the Army Air Corps, the Marine Corps, the Navy and Naval Reserves. Recipients were:

ADAMS, Lieutenant (jg) John P., U.S. Naval Reserve
ALLEN, Lieutenant Colonel Brooke E., U.S. Army
BARRETT
BOSELLEI
BURCH, Lieutenant Commander William O., Jr., U.S. Navy
CAPUTE, Private First Class Joseph, U.S. Army
CATARIUS
CHAPMAN
CLIFTON, Master Sergeant Benjamin, U.S. Army
COMPTON, Second Lieutenant William B., U.S. Army
DICKEY, Gunner Robert L., U.S. Marine Corps
DOBSON, Ensign Clee John, U.S. Navy
FAULKNER, Lieutenant Cecil L., U.S. Army
GRAY, Lieutenant James S., U.S. Navy
HEITMAN, Second Lieutenant Walter E., U.S. Army
JENNINGS, Master Sergeant Simpson L., U.S. Army
JOHNS, Private Robert, U.S. Army
KLEIN, Lieutenant (jg) Norman, U.S. Navy
KIGHT
KROEGER, Lieutenant Edwin J., U.S. Naval Reserve
McCUSKEY, Lieutenant Elbert S., U.S. Naval Reserve

MEHLE, Lieutenant R. W., U.S. Navy
MORAN
MUSTIAN, Second Lieutenant Thomas C., U.S. Army
O'BRIEN, Lieutenant Frank, U.S. Army
PARSONS, Corporal James C., U.S. Army
PECK
PETERSON, Commander John, U.S. Navy
RAWIE, Lieutenant Wilmer, U.S. Navy
SANDS
SOMERS, First Lieutenant Charles W., U.S. Marine Corps
*STERLING, Second Lieutenant Gordon H., U.S. Army
YARBROUGH, Lieutenant F. T., U.S. Army

* Posthumous award

CITATIONS FOR DISTINGUISHED FLYING CROSS

LIEUTENANT (jg) JOHN P. ADAMS, U.S. NAVAL RESERVES

"For heroically piloting his carrier fighter plane, a four-engined patrol bomber seaplane, into action against the enemy during the Gilbert Islands attack, and assisting in the destruction of a Japanese craft."

LIEUTENANT COLONEL BROOKE E. ALLEN, U.S. ARMY

Research has failed to reveal details of Colonel Brooke's heroism except for a listing with his name.

BARRETT
BOSELLEI

These two surnames are all that we have from a listing of recipients of the DFC.

LIEUTENANT COMMANDER WILLIAM O. BURCH, JR., U.S. NAVY

"As Commanding Officer of a scouting squadron, LCDR Burch led carrier planes against the Gilbert Islands on January 31, 1942 in a highly efficient manner. Personally, he made a direct hit on an enemy seaplane tender and sank a four engined patrol plane in the water by machine gun strafing."

PRIVATE FIRST CLASS JOSEPH CAPUTE, U.S. ARMY

"For execution of a hazardous and important mission over enemy territory, and for displaying heroism and extraordinary achievement while participating in an aerial flight mission of a highly secret nature."

CATARIUS
CHAPMAN

These two surnames are all that we have from a listing for DFC recipients.

MASTER SERGEANT BENJAMIN CLIFTON, U.S. ARMY

"For execution of a hazardous and important mission over enemy territory and for displaying heroism, and extraordinary achievement while participating in an aerial flight mission of a highly secret nature."

SECOND LIEUTENANT WILLIAM B. COMPTION, U.S. ARMY

"For execution of a hazardous and important mission over enemy territory and for displaying heroism, and extraordinary achievement while participating in an aerial flight mission of a highly secretive nature."

GUNNER ROBERT L. DICKEY, U.S. MARINE CORPS

"For heroic conduct in aerial combat with an enemy seaplane near Midway Island March 10, 1942. During the near approach of an enemy four-engined seaplane to the Island of Midway, Marine Gunner Dickey was the pilot of a fighting plane in a command which was ordered to intercept and destroy the enemy plane. Despite difficult aerial combat conditions because of heavy cloud formations, in which the enemy plane took full advantage in his evasive tactics, Marine Gunner Dickey pressed home his attack in an aggressive and effective manner which contributed to the destruction of the enemy four-engined seaplane, and, although wounded in the arm, maneuvered his plane safely to Midway Island. His action throughout was in accordance with the best traditions of the Naval Service."

ENSIGN CLEE JOHN DOBSON, U.S. NAVY

"For participation February 1, 1942 in the attack on the Marshall Islands. As a member of a Scouting Squadron Ensign Dobson participated in the initial attack on Kwajalein Atoll and in the subsequent attack on Wotje Harbor, Marshall Islands on February 1, 1942. His initiative and determination in the execution of these missions, effected in the face of enemy fighter opposition and heavy anti-aircraft fire, resulted in heavy losses to the enemy, including one fighter damaged in combat, one submarine sunk by a direct bomb hit and one auxiliary vessel damaged by a near miss. His courage and the effectiveness with which he accomplished his mission were in keeping with the best traditions of the naval service."

LIEUTENANT CECIL L. FAULKNER, U.S. ARMY

"For execution of a hazardous and important mission over enemy territory and for displaying heroism, and extraordinary achievement while participating in an aerial flight mission of highly secretive nature."

LIEUTENANT JAMES S. GRAY, U.S. NAVY

"On February 1, 1942 he led a bombing and strafing attack against Maloelap Islands in the face of a strong enemy aerial opposition. In the action that followed he shot down two enemy fighter planes."

SECOND LIEUTENANT WALTER E. HEITZMAN, U.S. ARMY

"For execution of a hazardous and important mission over enemy territory and for displaying heroism and extraordinary achievement while participating in an aerial flight mission of a highly secretive nature."

MASTER SERGEANT SIMPSON L. JENNINGS, U.S. ARMY

"For execution of a hazardous and important mission over enemy territory and for displaying heroism and extraordinary achievement while participating in an aerial flight mission of a highly secretive nature."

PRIVATE ROBERT JOHNS, U.S. ARMY

"For execution of a hazardous and important mission over enemy territory and for displaying heroism, and extraordinary achievement while participating in an aerial flight mission of a highly secretive nature."

LIEUTENANT (jg) NORMAN KLEIN, U.S. NAVY

"For participation February 1, 1942 in the attack on the Marshall Islands."

KIGHT

This is another case where all we could find was a single last name in a listing.

LIEUTENANT EDWIN J. KROEGER, U.S. NAVAL RESERVE

"Lt. Kroeger took part in the carrier-plane attack on Tarawa Island on February 1, 1942. Subsequently he was engaged by an enemy fighter and sustained a serious foot injury from the latters machinegun fire. Although unable to use that foot to control his plane, he managed to maneuver into position for his gunner to shoot down the Japanese attacker. Then, faint from loss of blood, he brought his craft safely back to the carrier."

LIEUTENANT ELBERT S. McCUSKEY, U.S. NAVAL RESERVE

"Lieutenant McCuskey took his carrier based fighter plane into combat against an enemy four-engined bomber seaplane during the action in the Gilbert Islands on January 31, 1942. He helped shoot down the craft that was attempting to attack his carrier."

LIEUTENANT R. W. MEHLE, U.S. NAVY

"For participation February 1, 1942 in the attack on the Marshall Islands. For distinguished service and heroic conduct in the line of his profession and heroic conduct in aerial flight as section leader of combat patrol VF-6. Upon intercepting an enemy twin float, single-engine seaplane, he immediately pressed home a determined offensive attack which resulted in the destruction of that plane. Later that same day, in company with two other pilots of his squadron, he intercepted and attacked two twin-engined bombers, and he assisted in the destruction of one and the damaging of the other."

MORAN

Another case of a lone last name in a listing of Distinguished Flying Cross recipients.

SECOND LIEUTENANT THOMAS C. MUSTAIN, U.S. ARMY

"For execution of a hazardous and important mission over enemy territory and for displaying heroism, and extraordinary achievement while participating in an aerial flight mission of a highly secretive nature."

LIEUTENANT FRANK O'BRIEN, U.S. ARMY

"As an Army Observer, Lt. O'Brien rescued a downed flyer on an ice flow near Alaska. The flyer, Lieutenant Elmer Booth, had parachuted from his disabled plane and had spent 24 hours on the ice."

CORPORAL JAMES C. PARSONS, U.S. ARMY

"For execution of a hazardous and important mission over enemy territory and for displaying heroism, and extraordinary achievement while participating in an aerial flight mission of a highly secretive nature."

PECK

Another case of a lone last name in a listing of Distinguished Flying Cross recipients.

COMMANDER JOHN PETERSON, U.S. NAVY

"As Commanding Officer of a Patrol Wing, Commander Peterson led his men and planes in 'miracles' of warfare performed during 90 days of fierce action against numerically superior Japanese forces in the southwest Pacific."

LIEUTENANT WILMER E. RAWIE, U.S. NAVY

"Lieutenant Rawie assisted in bombing and strafing Maloelap Islands on February 1, 1942 despite heavy enemy fighter and anti-aircraft opposition. In the ensuing action he downed a Japanese fighter plane."

SANDS

Without a first name or place and date of action, it was impossible to research details of Sand's heroism.

FIRST LIEUTENANT CHARLES W. SOMERS, U.S. MARINE CORPS

"For heroic conduct in aerial combat with an enemy sea plane near Midway Island on March 10, 1942. During the near approach of an enemy four-engined seaplane to the island of Midway, Lt. Somers, as pilot of a fighting plane in a command, was ordered to intercept and destroy the enemy plane. Despite difficult aerial combat conditions because of heavy cloud formations in which the enemy plane took full advantage in his evasive tactics, Lt. Somers pressed home his attack in an aggressive and effective manner which contributed to the destruction of the enemy four-engined seaplane. His action throughout was in accordance with the best traditions of the Naval Service."

*SECOND LIEUTENANT GORDON H. STERLING, U.S. ARMY

"When attached to the 46th Pursuit Squadron, 15th Pursuit Group (F), Air Corps, Lt. Sterling exhibited heroism and achievement while participating in an aerial engagement with Japanese airplanes over the water adjacent to the Island of Oahu on 7 December 1941. Lt. Sterling attacked an enemy airplane which was either damaged or destroyed as a result of his fire. While in the act of diving on this airplane Lt. Sterling was attacked from the rear by another enemy airplane and was shot down in flames resulting in his death."

LIEUTENANT F. T. YARBROUGH, U.S. ARMY

"As an Army Observer, Lieutenant Yarbrough assisted in rescuing a downed flyer on an ice flow near Alaska. The flyer, Lieutenant Elmer Booth, had parachuted from his disabled plane and had spent 24 hours on the ice."

* Posthumous award

Navy and Marine Corps Medal

NAVY AND MARINE CORPS MEDALS

By an Act of 1942, the Navy and Marine Corps Medal is presented to any person who, while serving in any capacity with the U.S. Navy or Marine Corps, shall have, since 6 December 1941, distinguished himself or herself by heroism and involving actual conflict with an enemy, or to any person to whom the Secretary of the Navy has formerly awarded a letter of commendation for heroism, regardless of date, subject to approval of the Board of Decorations and Medals. The saving of a life or the success of the voluntary heroic act is not essential to the award.

DESCRIPTION

The medal is octagonal in shape with a spread-winged eagle facing right, perched on a fouled anchor. Below the anchor is a globe depicting the western hemisphere and below that the inscription, "HEROISM."

The ribbon combines the colors of the Navy and Marine Corps, blue, gold and scarlet.

Each recipient in the following list received a Navy and Marine Corps Medal and the following Citation. (Following this list is a smaller group of individual Citations.)

"For devotion to duty as divers during the salvage of ships at Pearl Harbor immediately following the 7 December 1941 attack."

BENNETT, Carpenters Mate First Class Pryor, USN

BESTUL, Chief Shipfitter Morris C., USN

BLACKBURN, Carpenter Earl S., USN

BUSCH, Shipfitter First Class Frederick Davis, USN

BUSH, Shipfitter Second Class Frank Roy, USN

CARY, Shipfitter First Class Thomas, USN

DANIEL, Chief Gunners Mate Alfred Eugene, USN

DOVER, Gunners Mate First Class Nelson H., USN

Du BOIS, Shipfitter First Class Carl W., USN

FORLER, Boatswain Ralph E., USN

FRAZIER, Chief Gunner Glen, USN

GREEN, Gunners Mate Second Class James William, USN

HENDRICKS, Chief Shipfitter Harald F., USN

KATZENSTEIN, Chief Electricians Mate Alfred J., USN

LEWIS, Carpenters Mate First Class, Hugh D., USN

MAHAN, Machinist Mate First Class James R., USNR

MARTIN, Carpenter Jack Floyd, USNR
MULLEN, Chief Shipfitter Robert F., USN
PACITTI, Gunners Mate First Class Louis J., USN
PALMQUIST, Carpenters Mate First Class Glenn L., USN
PETERS, Carpenters Mate Christian R., USNR
ROBERTSON, Gunners Mate Second Class William Elmer, USN
ROCHE, Carpenters Mate First Class John J. Jr., USN
SAYLES, Shipfitter First Class Harry A., USN
THOMAS, Shipfitter First Class William Houston, USN
TINSLEY, Metalsmith First Class Kenneth F., USNR
VANDAGRIFF, Shipfitter First Class Tony G., USN
VAUGHN, Shipfitter First Class Herbert E., Jr., USNR
WEST, Boatswains Mate First Class Delbert L., USN
ZAKULEC, Shipfitter First Class Walter, USN

Also:

*BOATSWAIN ADOLPH MARCUS BOTHNE, U.S. NAVY

"During the salvage of the battleship **USS NEVADA,** Boatswain Bothne rescued two shipmates from a hydrogen sulfide filled compartment. Unfortunately both men were overcome and died from the poisonous fumes."

*LIEUTENANT JAMES STROUD CLARKSON, U.S. NAVY

"During the salvage of the battleship **USS NEVADA** Lt. Clarkson lost his life upon exposure to hydrogen sulfide gas fumes 7 February 1942."

*CHIEF WATER TENDER FRANCIS D. DAY, U.S. NAVY

"For assisting fifteen crew members to escape through a submerged porthole. He lost his own life in doing so."

*CHIEF MACHINIST MATE PETER C. DEVRIES, U.S. NAVY

"During the salvaging of the battleship **USS NEVADA,** Chief Machinist Mate Peter C. DeVries lost his life in an effort to save the life of Lieutenant James Stroud Clarkson 7 February 1942."

LIEUTENANT COMMANDER HOWARD E. HAYNES, U.S. NAVY (RET.)

"For outstanding performance of duty as Officer-in-charge of diving activities incident to the salvage of ships at Pearl Harbor after the attack by the Japanese."

ENSIGN ROBERT M. HENDON, U.S. NAVY

"For outstanding performance of duty as leading diver and later officer supervisor of divers during salvage operations at Pearl Harbor after the attack by the Japanese."

LIEUTENANT (jg) ROMAN G. MANTHEI, U.S. NAVY

"For outstanding performance of duty as Officer-in-charge of Ordnance Salvage Activities at Pearl Harbor after the attack by the Japanese Fleet."

*LIEUTENANT (jg) ALOYSIUS H. SCHMITT, CHAPLAIN CORPS, U.S. NAVY

"During the attack on the fleet by Japanese forces at Pearl Harbor, the battleship **USS OKLAHOMA** listed and turned over. Chaplain Aloysius H. Schmitt assisted shipmates to escape through a small porthole, remaining to the last and loosing his own life."

SHIPFITTER FIRST CLASS WILLIAM S. THOMAS, U.S. NAVY

"At the height of the attack on the Fleet by Japanese forces at Pearl Harbor, Shipfitter William S. Thomas rescued a Commander of the Medical Corps from the surf, bringing him safely to shore."

*CHIEF WATERTENDER PAUL R. WRIGHT, U.S. NAVAL RESERVE

"During the attack on the Fleet by Japanese forces at Pearl Harbor, Chief Watertender Paul R. Wright assisted shipmates to escape through a small porthole, remaining too long in the ship and loosing his own life."

* Posthumous awards

Bronze Star

BRONZE STAR

The Bronze Star is presented to any person serving with Army, Navy, Marine Corps or Coast Guard on or after 7 December 1941 who distinguishes himself by heroic or meritorious achievement or service, and/or involving participation in aerial flight, in connection with military or naval operations against an enemy.

The Bronze Star is exactly what its name says it is, a star made of bronze. In the center is a smaller star; ridges characterize each of the star's sections.

Only three Bronze Stars were awarded for this time, two of them posthumously. Recipients were:

ASHER, Ensign Nathan Frederick, U.S. Navy

*SIMENSEN, Second Lieutenant Carleton E., U.S. Marine Corps

*TURNER, Private William G., U.S. Marine Corps

BRONZE STAR WITH COMBAT "V"

ENSIGN NATHAN FREDERICK ASHER, U.S. NAVY

"For heroic service while attached to the **USS BLUE** during the enemy Japanese air raid on Pearl Harbor, Territory of Hawaii on 7 December 1941. Acting as senior officer, Asher took his ship to sea under fire and operated offshore in a most efficient manner. His initiative and leadership were in keeping with the highest traditions of the United States Naval Service."

NOTE: Ensign Asher's award of Bronze Star is an upgrade from a Letter of Commendation from Secretary of Navy Frank Knox.

*SECOND LIEUTENANT CARLETON E. SIMENSEN, U.S. MARINE CORPS

"For heroic service while attached to the **USS ARIZONA** during the enemy Japanese air raid on Pearl Harbor, T.H., 7 December 1941. Remaining cool and courageous despite violent explosions and raging fires, 2nd Lt. Simensen was largely instrumental in quelling the momentary panic resulting from the surprise attack. The first Marine to start up the long ladders leading to his station in the mainmast, he proceeded steadily in the face of heavy bombing and hostile machine gun attacks. Killed instantly by hostile fire upon reaching the searchlight platform, 2nd Lt.

Simensen, by his initiative and leadership, served as an inspiring example of heroism, and his devotion to duty was in keeping with the highest traditions of the U.S. Naval Service. He gallantly gave his life for his country."

*PRIVATE WILLIAM G. TURNER, U.S. MARINE CORPS

"For heroic achievement while serving with Marine Scout Bombing Squadron 231 in action against enemy Japanese forces at Oahu, Hawaiian Islands on 7 December 1941. When the Ewa Flying Field was subjected to a fierce attack by Japanese aircraft, Private Turner repeatedly defied gunfire from the hostile planes to assist in supplying ammunition to the operator of a friendly machine gun and continued in his courageous efforts until subsequently wounded by a blast of enemy fire. His initiative and perseverance were in keeping with the highest traditions of the United States Naval Service."

NOTE: The above two awards, presented to parents October 1947 and May 1947 respectively, were up-grades from Letters of Commendation, Simensen's from Secretary of Navy Frank Knox, Turner's from CINCPACFLT Admiral Chester W. Nimitz, USN.

* Posthumous awards

Purple Heart

PURPLE HEART

On 7 December 1941 neither Navy, Marine Corps nor Coast Guard personnel were eligible for the Purple Heart. Only members of the Army and Army Air Corps could receive that decoration. However, Navy, Marine and Coast Guard members may have been awarded this medal if they had been attached to an Army command on the occasion of the Japanese attack.

Several months into 1942, new regulations, backdated to 7 December, allowed seagoing service members to receive the Purple Heart. More regulations authorized all services to become eligible for the Silver Star, Bronze Star and Legion of Merit. The Medal of Merit and Medal of Freedom were created at a later date to cover civilian heroism.

To determine the number and names of those who were eligible and those who received the Purple Heart would be a tremendous task, one which the authors knew might be impossible to complete accurately and would delay publication beyond the value of the results.

The Purple Heart is awarded to persons wounded in action against the enemy of the United States while serving with the Armed Forces as a result of act of such enemy, if wound necessitated treatment by medical officer. Also to next of kin of person killed in action.

The Purple Heart is often considered the most beautiful medal. The obverse contains a side view of the head and shoulders of George Washington in raised white enamel on a purple enameled background surrounded by a border of white enamel. On the upper part of the heart from which the ribbon is suspended there is a shield of white and purple enamel containing three stars in purple on a white background and two horizontal purple stripes. On either side of the shield is inscribed FOR MILITARY MERIT. The medal is suspended from a ribbon of purple with narrow white edge.

UNIT CITATIONS

An Executive Order of 6 February 1942 provided for the awarding of a Presidential Citation to any ship, aircraft or naval unit, any marine aircraft detachment or higher unit for outstanding performance in action on or after 16 October 1941.

A General Order of February 3, 1943 authorized a similar provision for all Army units.

Coincidentally, the Commander-in-Chief of the U.S. Pacific Fleet was authorized to award citations in his name to any military unit within his command for outstanding performance in action on or after 7 December 1941.

There is no medal for the Unit Citation. Instead, each recipient is privileged to wear a campaign ribbon representing the Citation; and, the unit is entitled to paint an enlarged version of the ribbon on their ship, aircraft or building. The colors of the ribbon are red, blue and gold, arranged horizontally.

PRESIDENTIAL CITATION

The President of the United States to the Wake detachment of the 1st Defense Battalion, United States Marine Corps, under command of Major James P. S. Devereaux, United States Marines

and

the Marine Fighting Squadron 211 of Marine Aircraft Group 21, under command of Major Paul A. Putnam, United States Marines.

"The courageous conduct of the officers and men of these units, who defended Wake Island against an overwhelming superiority of enemy air, sea and land attacks from December 8 to 22, 1941, has been noted with admiration by their fellow countrymen and the civilized world, and will not be forgotten so long as gallantry and heroism are respected and honored. These units are commended for their devotion to duty and splendid conduct at their battle stations under most adverse conditions. With limited defensive means against attacks in great force, they manned their shore installations and flew their aircraft so well that five enemy warships were either sunk or severely damaged, many hostile planes shot down and an unknown number of land troops destroyed."

NOTE: Civilian contract personnel were under control of Wake Island Commanding Officer Commander Winfield E. Cunningham, U.S. Navy.

Many of these men fought alongside the Marines, dying with their brothers in uniform or becoming prisoners of war.

The above citation was signed by Franklin D. Roosevelt, President of the United States.

CITATIONS FROM COMMANDER-IN-CHIEF, UNITED STATES PACIFIC FLEET

The Commander-in-Chief, United States Pacific Fleet, takes pleasure in commending the UNITED STATES NAVAL HOSPITAL, PEARL HARBOR, TERRITORY OF HAWAII, for service as set forth in the following CITATION:

"For meritorious achievement and distinguished service subsequent to the Japanese Air Attack on the United States Fleet at Pearl Harbor, T.H., on December 7, 1941. At the time of the attack and afterwards, this unit displayed conspicuous devotion in the line of duty. Its ability to cope with this disaster was responsible for the successful care of all casualties and the saving of many lives. The professional skill displayed and distinguished service rendered by this Hospital Unit were in keeping with the highest traditions of the naval service."

(Signed) C. W. Nimitz,
Admiral, USN

NOTE: Captain Reynolds Hayden, Medical Corps, USN, was in command of the Naval Hospital at Pearl Harbor at the time of the Japanese attack on December 7, 1941.

The Commander-in-Chief, United States Pacific Fleet, takes pleasure in commending **USS SOLACE** for service as set forth in the following CITATION:

"For meritorious achievement and distinguished service during and subsequent to the Japanese air attack on the United States Fleet at Pearl Harbor, T.H., on 7 December, 1941. At the time of the attack and afterwards, this unit displayed conspicuous devotion in the line of duty. Its ability to cope with this disaster was responsible for the successful care of all casualties and the saving of many lives. The professional skill displayed and distinguished service rendered by this hospital ship were in keeping with the highest traditions of the naval service."

(Signed) C. W. Nimitz
Admiral, USN

The Commander-in-Chief, United States Pacific Fleet, takes pleasure in commending: WHEELER FIELD FIRE DEPARTMENT, CHIEF ROSS I. EWING, WHEELER'S FIRE CHIEF, for service as set forth in the following CITATION:

"For gallant conduct under fire during the Japanese Air Attack on Wheeler Field on December 7, 1941. The men of the Wheeler Field Fire Department stayed at their posts and, at risk of lives, performed necessary tasks in exemplary manner."

(Signed) C. W. Nimitz
Admiral, USN

Medal for Merit (non-military)

MEDALS AWARDED TO CIVILIANS

A SPECIAL VALOR MEDAL, comparable to the Distinguished Service Medal, and a Commendatory letter from President Franklin D. Roosevelt to:
ALICE BECKLEY SPENCER, civilian telephone supervisor at Naval Air Station, Kaneohe Bay, Territory of Hawaii.

"For distinguished devotion to duty, extraordinary courage, most efficient action, and utter disregard of her personal safety during the Japanese assault on the Naval Air Station, Kaneohe Bay. At the height of the attack, she arrived at her post, relieved an enlisted man and remained at the switchboard throughout the day, under enemy fire. Her tireless service in plain view of hundreds of officers and men passing through the building was considered to have been a steadying influence in no small degree, and furnished an example conforming to the best traditions of the service."

A SPECIAL MEDAL FOR DISTINGUISHED SERVICE, and Letter of Commendation from Secretary of Navy, Frank Knox, to:
HENRY R. DANNER, civilian machinist at Pearl Harbor Shipyard.

"Working in a drydock when the enemy attack began, he went on board a battleship when a shortage of men in her gun crews became apparent, and assisted in the ammunition supply. Later, while he was packing the stern tube of a ship so she could be undocked, working without lights, a heavy piece of machinery fell and broke his foot. Despite his injury, because of the emergency, he completed the task and carried on for five days until, owing to pain, he was unable to work."

MEDAL OF MERIT

DESCRIPTION

The obverse of this medal bears an eagle resting on a sheaf of arrows encircled by a blue enamel ring with thirteen stars. Bordering the arrows is the motto "Novus Ordo Seclorum," meaning the beginning of a New American Era, taken from the reverse of the Great Seal of the United States. The Medal is suspended from the ribbon by a green laurel wreath.

The reverse carries the words, "United States of American" and "For Merit," with the back of the eagle modeled.

CITATIONS FOR MEDAL OF MERIT

VERA M. JONES
"As Chief telephone operator at Pearl Harbor Navy Yard, Vera M. Jones remained at her post during the Japanese attack on Pearl Harbor, and thereafter for 24 hours."

HAWILA KALEOHANO
"On the small island of Niihau, most westerly of the main Hawaiian group, Hawila Kaleohano singlehandedly disarmed and captured a Japanese pilot who had crash landed his plane near Kaleohano's home. Kaleohano rowed to Kauai, sixteen hours away, for help. Upon his return he found that another native Hawaiian had killed the pilot."

BENEHAKAKA KANAHELE
"On the small island of Niihau, Benehakaka Kanahele and his wife were taken hostage by a Japanese pilot who had persuaded an American citizen of Japanese descent to help him terrorize the isolated village. When the pilot turned his back, Kanahele managed to grab him by the neck and dash his head against a stone wall, killing him."

CIVILIAN FIRE CHIEF WILLIAM L. BENEDICT
"For organizing and directing Honolulu and Hickam Field firemen during the bombing and fires at Hangar 7, Hickam Field, and elsewhere."

LETTERS OF COMMENDATION

A salute to those men, regular Navy, Reserves and Marine Corps, who were awarded Letters of Commendation from the Secretary of the Navy, Frank Knox, and CINCPACFLT Admiral Chester W. Nimitz, USN, in recognition of their positive actions in defense of their country on the first day of World War II.

SECNAV honored 33 men; nine of these gave their lives while performing at their duty stations. CINCPACFLT singled out 226; most of these recipients lived to read their letters.

Their brave acts ranged from rescuing trapped personnel on ships to seeking out the enemy in lightly armed planes. Some men, in herculean efforts, shoved burning aircraft out of harm's way: others insured fast and accurate communication in the face of enemy fire; one man became a target when climbing a smokestack to repair an antenna. The acts of selflessness were almost as varied as their numbers.

LETTERS OF COMMENDATION FROM CINCPACFLT
(Chief Naval Forces Pacific Fleet)

"For caring for many wounded men from Naval Air Station Pearl Harbor and nearby disabled ships, and thereby assisting most ably in the face of enemy bombing and strafing."

ANDERSON, C.K., PHARMACIST MATE THIRD CLASS, USN
ARCHER, J.R., PHARMACIST MATE THIRD CLASS, USN
ARNOLD, WALTER F., LIEUTENANT (MEDICAL CORPS) USNR
AUBREY, W.G., PHARMACIST MATE SECOND CLASS, USN
BOYD, W.R., PHARMACIST MATE SECOND CLASS, USN
BROWNING, G.F., PHARMACIST MATE THIRD CLASS, USN
CANON, RUSH L., LIEUTENANT (DENTAL CORPS), USN
CANTERBURY, JR., J.V., PHARMACIST MATE SECOND CLASS, USN
CAVENY, ELMER L., LIEUTENANT (MEDICAL CORPS), USN
CRAWFORD, V.G., PHARMACIST MATE FIRST CLASS, USN
CRAWFORD, T.L., PHARMACIST MATE SECOND CLASS, USN
CUNNINGHAM, J.G., SEAMAN SECOND CLASS, USN

DEVERE, W.H., PHARMACIST MATE THIRD CLASS, USN
EVERETT, A.R., PHARMACIST MATE THIRD CLASS, USN
FIECHEL, K.O., PHARMACIST MATE SECOND CLASS, USN
GRIFFITH, EUGENE, CHIEF PHARMACIST MATE, USN
HARP, R.C., PHARMACIST MATE THIRD CLASS, USN
LAMPRECHT, S.M., PHARMACIST MATE SECOND CLASS
LONGWAY, KENNETH L., LIEUTENANT (jg) (DENTAL CORPS),
  USN
MINGER, C.R., PHARMACIST MATE SECOND CLASS, USN
MORGAN, H.D., PHARMACIST MATE FIRST CLASS, USN
MORRIS, C.L., PHARMACIST MATE SECOND CLASS, USN
NICHOLSON, W.F., PHARMACIST MATE FIRST CLASS, USN
PETH, R.J., PHARMACIST MATE SECOND CLASS, USN
PRENTICE, G.R., PHARMACIST MATE SECOND CLASS, USN
READ, D.D., PHARMACIST MATE THIRD CLASS, USN
RINEHART, R.O., PHARMACIST MATE THIRD CLASS
SCHUESSLER, ELMER W., LIEUTENANT (DENTAL CORPS),
  USNR
SHERRARD, P.J., PHARMACIST MATE FIRST CLASS, USN
SMITH, F., PHARMACIST MATE SECOND CLASS, USN
SMITH, JAROUD B., LIEUTENANT (jg) (MEDICAL CORPS), USN
STEVENS, Jr., C.E., PHARMACIST MATE SECOND CLASS,
  USN
WEST, RODNEY T., LIEUTENANT (jg) (MEDICAL CORPS), USN
WHITE, E., PHARMACIST MATE SECOND CLASS, USN

The following signalmen in the Navy Yard signal tower were cited "for insuring fast and accurate communication between the Commander-in-Chief and ships of the fleet although exposed to severe enemy strafing and bombing attack."

ADAMS, V.L., RADIOMAN THIRD CLASS, USN
BROWN, J.L., SIGNALMAN FIRST CLASS, USN
CLARK, C.B., CHIEF SIGNALMAN, USN
CROUTHERS, C.F., SIGNALMAN THIRD CLASS, USN
DECKER, G.F., SIGNALMAN SECOND CLASS, USN
EDWARDS, C.B., SIGNALMAN THIRD CLASS, USN
GORDON, J.T., SIGNALMAN FIRST CLASS, USN
GOSTEL, J., SIGNALMAN SECOND CLASS, USN
HOUGHTON, A.J., SIGNALMAN THIRD CLASS, USN

HURST, R.W., SIGNALMAN SECOND CLASS, USN
KYLE, W.B., SIGNALMAN FIRST CLASS, USN
MARTIN, R.D., SIGNALMAN FIRST CLASS, USN
MERRITT, J.D., SIGNALMAN THIRD CLASS, USN
MILLER, R.C., SIGNALMAN FIRST CLASS, USN
NYGREN, D.L., SIGNALMAN FIRST CLASS, USN
PALMER, R.Q. SIGNALMAN FIRST CLASS, USN
PRYOR, W., CHIEF SIGNALMAN, USN
RABE, E.W., SIGNALMAN SECOND CLASS, USN
SCOGGINS, W.B., SIGNALMAN THIRD CLASS, USN
SEIFERT, R.E., SIGNALMAN FIRST CLASS, USN
STEVENS, L.J., SIGNALMAN SECOND CLASS, USN
THEOBALD, L.L., SEAMAN FIRST CLASS, USN
TRIMBUR, A.F., SIGNALMAN THIRD CLASS, USN
VYSKOCIL, J.A., SIGNALMAN THIRD CLASS, USN
WARNER, W., SEAMAN FIRST CLASS, USN

"For participation as color guard at Naval Air Station, Pearl Harbor. While awaiting morning colors when the enemy struck on 7 December 1941, nevertheless assisted in the ceremony with the same smartness and precision which characterized their participation in that ceremony in peace time, despite the severe enemy bombing and strafing at the station."

DUDOVIC, FRANK, PRIVATE, USMC
YOUNG, J.D., PRIVATE, USMC
ZELLER, P.O., PRIVATE, USMC

"For fighting fires and rescuing trapped personnel below decks on the battleship, **USS OKLAHOMA**."

BROOKS, W.M., MESS ATTENDANT FIRST CLASS, USN
CAMPBELL, E.R., CHIEF ELECTRICIANS MATE, USN
CANFIELD, R.B., ENSIGN, USN
FAIN, E.M., ENSIGN, USN
GUNNELS, C.W., ENSIGN, USN
HALL, B.C., ENSIGN, USN
HALL, C.H., ENSIGN, USN
KIRKPATRICK, R.D., ENSIGN, USN
LYDEN, C.J., ENSIGN, USNR
McGRATH, T.P., ENSIGN, USN

NICOLSON, A.T., ENSIGN, USN
PRICE, E.V., CHIEF ELECTRICIANS MATE, USN
RUDDEN, T.J., ENSIGN, USN
SETTLE, R.L., ENSIGN, USN
WALKER, W.W., ENSIGN, USN

"For rescue of personnel trapped below decks of a battleship."

ALFORD, L.B., ELECTRICIANS MATE FIRST CLASS, USN
BELDEN, E.W., MACHINIST MATE FIRST CLASS, USN
BEZVODA, S.F., ELECTRICIANS MATE FIRST CLASS, USN
BLY, C.L., MACHINIST MATE FIRST CLASS, USN
CHAMPION, C.H., ENSIGN, USN
COON, R.V., ELECTRICIANS MATE THIRD CLASS, USN
EBBERSON, L.F., FIREMAN THIRD CLASS, USN
FLEMING, C.H., MACHINIST MATE SECOND CLASS, USN
FRANCK, D.E., ELECTRICIANS MATE THIRD CLASS, USN
GALIJEAN, C.W., FIREMAN THIRD CLASS, USN
GAROUTTE, H.J., FIREMAN FIRST CLASS, USN
GREENBAUM, H., ELECTRICIANS MATE THIRD CLASS, USN
ILIAN, E., ELECTRICIANS MATE FIRST CLASS, USN
ISENHOUR, R.A., MACHINIST MATE SECOND CLASS, USN
KOEPPLINGER, C.F., BOATSWAINS MATE SECOND CLASS,
  USN
LABARRE, C.A., ENSIGN, USNR
LEWIS, W.A.J., ENSIGN, USN
LITZ, C.L., ELECTRICIANS MATE THIRD CLASS, USN
MAXWELL, G.R., ELECTRICIANS MATE FIRST CLASS, USN
MILLER, R.W., CHIEF ELECTRICIAN, USN
MINCKLEY, R.F., ELECTRICIANS MATE SECOND CLASS, USN
NUNNELLEY, L.E., FIREMAN THIRD CLASS, USN
PLUARD, F.D., FIREMAN THIRD CLASS, USN
ROUNTREE, W.H., FIREMAN FIRST CLASS, USN
SAMUEL, H., FIREMAN THIRD CLASS, USN
STREETER, C.L., ELECTRICIANS MATE SECOND CLASS, USN
TAYLOR, L.A., ENSIGN, USNR
ROTH, F.J., FIREMAN SECOND CLASS, USN
WAITE, J.E., ELECTRICIANS MATE THIRD CLASS, USN

"For prompt and efficient action and utter disregard of personal danger in the effort to repel the attack on Naval Air Station, Kaneohe Bay, Oahu on 7 December, 1941 at the time of the Japanese attack on that installation."

*BROWN, W.S., AVIATION MACHINIST MATE SECOND CLASS, USN

*BUCKLEY, J.D., AVIATION ORDNANCEMAN THIRD CLASS, USN

BYRON, HARRY G., AVIATION CHIEF MACHINIST MATE, USN

*FORMOE, C.M., AVIATION MACHINIST MATE FIRST CLASS, USN

*FOSS, R.S., ENSIGN, USNR

*FOX, JR., LEE, ENSIGN, USNR

*GRIFFIN, D.T., AVIATION MACHINIST MATE FIRST CLASS, USN

*INGRAM, G.W., SEAMAN SECOND CLASS, USN

*LAWRENCE, CHARLES, AVIATION MACHINIST MATE SECOND CLASS, USN

*MANNING, M.C., AVIATION MACHINIST MATE THIRD CLASS, USN

McCORMACK, J.J., LIEUTENANT, USN

*NEWMAN, L.G., AVIATION MACHINIST MATE THIRD CLASS, USN

*OTTERSTETTER, C.W., SEAMAN SECOND CLASS, USN

*PORTERFIELD, R.K., AVIATION MACHINIST MATE THIRD CLASS, USN

*ROBINSON, J.H., SEAMAN SECOND CLASS, USN

*SMART, J.G., ENSIGN, USNR

*UHLMAN, R.W., ENSIGN, USNR

WALLACE, M.R., ENSIGN, USNR

*WATSON, R.A., AVIATION MACHINIST MATE FIRST CLASS, USN

*WEAVER, L.D., SEAMAN FIRST CLASS, USN

"For saving three aircraft and a barracks from destruction during the bombing and strafing at the Naval Air Station, Pearl Harbor."

AMIS, H.B., COXSWAIN, USN

BRATTON, R.R., SEAMAN SECOND CLASS, USN

BURNFIL, JOHN, CHIEF BOATSWAIN MATE, USN
CLICK, D.H., SEAMAN FIRST CLASS, USN
DINAPOLI, ANTONIO, SEAMAN FIRST CLASS, USN
DOHERTY, D.J., SEAMAN FIRST CLASS, USN
EVANS, F.S., SEAMAN SECOND CLASS, USN
FERRIN, J.L., SEAMAN SECOND CLASS, USN
MILLIGAN, E.C., SEAMAN FIRST CLASS, USN
PRUITT, JR., P.E., SEAMAN SECOND CLASS, USN
SWISHER, B.L., SEAMAN FIRST CLASS, USN
WORTHEN, W.E., SEAMAN FIRST CLASS, USN

"The following airmen volunteered to serve as pilots, co-pilots and crew members of utility planes to seek out the enemy with only Springfield rifles or low caliber machineguns as armament:

ASHWORTH, P.W., AVIATION MACHINIST MATE THIRD
CLASS, USN
BAKER, L.J., SEAMAN SECOND CLASS, USN
BIRMINGHAM, J.A., SEAMAN SECOND CLASS, USN
BYRD, W.P., AVIATION MACHINIST MATE, USN
DOREN, A., AVIATION CHIEF MACHINIST MATE, USN
EVANS, W.R., AVIATION MACHINIST FIRST CLASS, USN
FAUBER, R.S., AVIATION MACHINIST MATE FIRST CLASS,
USN
FRISSEL, E.L., AVIATION MACHINIST MATE THIRD CLASS,
USN
GALLUPE, A.P., AVIATION MACHINIST MATE FIRST CLASS,
USN
GEISE, E.C., AVIATION MACHINIST MATE SECOND CLASS,
USN
GEISE, E.C., AVIATION CHIEF MACHINIST MATE, USN
GLASSER, F.W., RADIOMAN THIRD CLASS, USN
JOHNSON, J.H., AVIATION MACHINIST MATE SECOND
CLASS, USN
KAMMERER, L.A., AVIATION MACHINIST MATE FIRST
CLASS, USN
KARR, E.V., RADIOMAN THIRD CLASS, USN
LESHER, D.J., AVIATION MACHINIST MATE FIRST CLASS, USN
ROSE, J.J., SHIPS COOK THIRD CLASS, USN
SCHULTZ, W.G., RADIOMAN THIRD CLASS, USN

SIMPSON, W.H., AVIATION MACHINIST MATE FIRST CLASS, USN
SWITZER, D. LEE, AVIATION MACHINIST MATE FIRST CLASS, USN
WIDENER, G.F., AVIATION MACHINIST MATE SECOND CLASS, USN
WRIGHT, D.H., AVIATION CHIEF MACHINIST MATE, USN

"For various deeds of heroism, devotion to duty, efficient action and presence of mind."

ADAMS, J.W., JR., LIEUTENANT COMMANDER, USN
ADKINS, L.W., CHIEF BOATSWAIN, USN
ANDERSON, H.C., ENSIGN, USNR
APPLEGATE, H.A., PAY CLERK, USN
BALDWIN, H.J., MACHINIST MATE FIRST CLASS, USN
BALFOUR, A.J., RADIOMAN THIRD CLASS, USN
BEACH, F., CHIEF MACHINIST, USN
BENEFIELD, O.W., RADIOMAN THIRD CLASS, USN
BIESZCZ, R.R., SEAMAN FIRST CLASS, USN
BRANDT, P.M., BOILERMAN FIRST CLASS, USN
BRENERMANN, H.L., SERGEANT, USMC
CAMPBELL, COLIN, COMMANDER, USN
CANN, P.W., LIEUTENANT, USN
CRADOCK, H.E., CHIEF GUNNERS MATE, USN
D'AMELLIO, J.A., SEAMAN FIRST CLASS, USN
DAY, CHARLES E., RADIOMAN THIRD CLASS, USN
DORSETT, H.C., SEAMAN FIRST CLASS, USN
EASTMAN, H.C., ANDERSON, ENSIGN, USNR
EKBLOM, A.R., CHIEF CARPENTERS MATE, USN
ERLY, E.B., LIEUTENANT, USN
FLECK, JR., F.E., LIEUTENANT, USN
GEISER, A.J., SEAMAN FIRST CLASS, USN
HALL, E.S., AVIATION ORDNANCE MAN THIRD CLASS, USN
HARDON, G.S., CHIEF TORPEDOMAN, USN
HARPER, J.S., LIEUTENANT COMMANDER, USN
HART, E.V., SEAMAN FIRST CLASS, USN
HAUCK, P.F., LIEUTENANT, USN
HAYES, H.R., COMMANDER, USN (RET.)
HELM, T.W., RADIOMAN THIRD CLASS, USN

HOLZHAUS, R.L., BOILERMAKER FIRST CLASS, USN
JACKSON, J.O., RADIOMAN SECOND CLASS, USN
KABLE, D.M., ENSIGN, USN
KENDALL, J.E., ENSIGN, USNR
KERR, T.E., AVIATION ORDNANCEMAN FIRST CLASS, USN
KOVALSIK, W.F., BOILERMAN FIRST CLASS, USN
KWOLIK, E.T., FIREMAN SECOND CLASS, USN
LANDRETH, J.L., ENSIGN, USN
LARRICK, G.W., CHIEF BOILERMAN, USN
*MILLER, W.C., RADIOMAN FIRST CLASS, USN
MOSHER, J.H., CHIEF WATER TENDER, USN
MOYER, B.D., ENSIGN, USNR
MULLINGS, J.H., MACHINIST MATE FIRST CLASS, USN
NICODEMUS, JR., G.K., ENSIGN, USNR
PAVLIN, B.F., ELECTRICIANS MATE THIRD CLASS, USN
PERUCCI, A.D., AVIATION ORDNANCEMAN FIRST CLASS,
  USN
POSTELTHWAITE, P.O., SEAMAN SECOND CLASS, USN
RAIDY, J.M., CHIEF ELECTRICIANS MATE, USN
RAU, JR., A.F., SEAMAN FIRST CLASS, USN
REORDAN, C.D., CAPTAIN, USN
RILEY, J.B., CHIEF BOATSWAIN MATE, USN
ROBBLEE, J.T., RADIOMAN FIRST CLASS, USN
ROSE, A.F., GUNNERS MATE THIRD CLASS, USN
SAFRANSKI, S.F., MACHINIST MATE FIRST CLASS, USN
SEARS, H.W., ENSIGN, USNR
SHORT, L.V., SEAMAN FIRST CLASS, USN
SIMMONS, O.L., RADIOMAN FIRST CLASS, USN
SPEAR, W.R., LIEUTENANT, USN (RET.)
STRATTON, J.T., CHIEF BOATSWAIN MATE, USN
THOMAS, W.S., ENSIGN, USNR
TRIPPENSEE, B.E.S., LIEUTENANT, USN
•TURNER, WILLIAM G., PRIVATE, USMC
WHITE, C.S., CAPTAIN, USMC
WILLIAMS, C.E., YEOMAN SECOND CLASS, USN
ZUBER, ADOLPH, MAJOR, USMC

* Indicates posthumous award
• Indicates up-grade; this one to Bronze Star with Combat "V"

LETTERS OF COMMENDATION
FROM
SECRETARY OF NAVY, FRANK KNOX

*ENSIGN N.F. ASHER, U.S. NAVY

"For showing extraordinary courage and disregard of his own safety. As acting commanding officer of a destroyer, he took his ship to sea under fire and operated off shore in a most efficient manner."
NOTE: Later upgraded to a Bronze Star with Combat "V".

CHIEF YEOMAN R.M. BALDWIN, U.S. NAVY

"For showing extraordinary courage and disregard of his own safety while the damage control officer of his battleship was commanding the vessel, by performing the latter's duties in an outstanding manner."

ENSIGN G.G. BALL, U.S. NAVY

"For showing extraordinary courage and disregard of his own safety. With two naval reserve Ensigns, he took a destroyer to sea, swept for magnetic mines near the harbor entrance, and performed ably until relieved by his regular commanding officer."

AVIATION ORDNANCEMAN FIRST CLASS M.J. CAPARREILL, U.S. NAVY

"For showing extraordinary courage and disregard of his own safety. At Naval Air Station, Kaneohe, he set up and operated a machine gun continuously in an exposed position despite heavy bombing and strafing."

ENSIGN S. CAPLAN, U.S. NAVY RESERVES

"As senior officer present on a destroyer, having been at sea a total of only eight months, he took his ship to sea and operated ably for 36 hours."

RADIOMAN FIRST CLASS J.T. CROWNOVER, U.S. NAVY

"For showing extraordinary courage and disregard of his own safety when he manned a machinegun at Naval Air Station, Kaneohe, until seriously wounded by shrapnel which resulted in the loss of his left eye."

ENSIGN E.T. DEACON, U.S. NAVY

"For showing extraordinary courage and disregard of his own safety. Returning in his scout plane to Pearl Harbor, he saw smoke, groups of Japanese planes and then attempted to land at Luke Field. Attacked by enemy fighters he thereupon sought to enter Hickam Field, but lost power when his engine was hit. Stalling into the water just short of the army air base, he found himself under rifle fire from the beach. He and his radioman were wounded. He bandaged the latter's arm, broke out the life raft, then paddled ashore."

*BOATSWAINS MATE SECOND CLASS S.M. GANTNER, U.S. NAVY

"For showing extraordinary courage and disregard of his own safety. As an antiaircraft gun captain he fought his weapon in local control, despite heavy casualties in his crew, exploding ammunition on deck and serious fires, until killed at his station."

*SEAMAN SECOND CLASS T.H. GARY, U.S. NAVY

"For showing extraordinary courage and disregard of his own safety. He helped rescue the injured on his battleship and in so doing gave up his own life."

AVIATION CHIEF ORDNANCEMAN L.A. GRISHAM, U.S. NAVY

"For showing extraordinary courage and disregard of his own safety when he took charge of supplying ammunition to machineguns in exposed positions at Naval Air Station, Kaneohe, until his left leg was blown off by an enemy bomb explosion."

CHIEF BOATSWAIN MATE JANSEN, U.S. NAVY

"For courage, as commanding officer of barge YG17, in going alongside one burning battleship, fighting flames despite exploding shells, then moving to another to execute the same dangerous task."

*ENSIGN I.W. JEFFERY, U.S. NAVY

"For showing extraordinary courage and disregard of his own safety when he organized a party and attempted by hand to maintain an ammunition supply to antiaircraft guns of his battleship."

RADIOMAN FIRST CLASS R.E. JONES, U.S. NAVY

"For showing extraordinary courage and disregard of his own safety. Along with Radioman Second Class J.G. Raines, he rescued one man and tried to save another trapped in a flame and smoke filled transmitter room on a patrol plane tender."

ENSIGN R.G. KELLY, U.S. NAVY RESERVE

"For showing extraordinary courage and disregard of his own safety. Although injured, he continued to direct a repair party, helped bring a fire under control and aided in removing dead and injured from a patrol plane tender."

*BOATSWAIN MATE SECOND CLASS K.T. LAMONS, U.S. NAVY

"For showing extraordinary courage and disregard of his own safety. As an antiaircraft gun captain, he fought his weapon in local control, despite heavy casualties in his crew, exploding ammunition on deck and serious fires, until killed at his station."

CHIEF QUARTERMASTER F.H. LEMMON, U.S. NAVAL RESERVE

"For showing extraordinary courage and disregard for his own safety. As chief master at arms, Naval Air Station, Pearl Harbor, he organized his small force and most ably handled the tremendous problem immediately presented."

RADIOMAN SECOND CLASS FRED M. LLEWELLYN, U.S. NAVY

"For showing extraordinary courage and disregard of his own safety. He remained in a burning hangar at Naval Air Station, Kaneohe, serving ammunition to machine guns until receiving serious injuries including loss of one eye in a bomb explosion."

AVIATION MACHINIST MATE FIRST CLASS DALE S. LYONS, U.S. NAVY

"For showing extraordinary courage and disregard of his own safety, in remaining in a burning hangar at Naval Air Station, Kaneohe, serving ammunition to machine guns until his left foot was severed in a bomb explosion."

LIEUTENANT COMMANDER B.E. MANSEAU, U.S. NAVY

"For showing extraordinary courage and disregard of his own safety. He assisted in having the drydocks flooded, then issued radio broadcast orders for all required navy yard workers to report for immediate duty. His initiative, coolness and efficiency inspired those about him."

RADIOMAN FIRST CLASS H.E. McCORMICK, U.S. NAVY

"For showing extraordinary courage and disregard of his own safety when he organized and led a repair party to restore the shotaway antenna at Naval Air Station, Pearl Harbor, climbing a high smokestack under fire to complete his work."

CHIEF GUNNERS MATE M.L. MILLARD, U.S. NAVY

"For showing extraordinary courage and disregard of his own safety when he cleared a loading casualty on a destroyer after sending the remainder of the weapon's crew from the gun and handling room."

YEOMAN FIRST CLASS KENTON NASH, U.S. NAVY

"For showing extraordinary courage and disregard of his own safety when he drove his car at Naval Air Station, Kaneohe, to a machine-gun position to lend assistance. As he stepped from his vehicle, his left arm was blown off by a bomb explosion."

*SEAMAN FIRST CLASS W.F. NEUDORF, U.S. NAVY

"For showing extraordinary courage and disregard of his own safety in controlling the antiaircraft gun, of which he was captain, in an outstanding manner until he was killed at his station on board a battleship."

BOATSWAIN S. OSMON, U.S. NAVY

"For showing extraordinary courage and disregard of his own safety. Although injured, he remained at his post on a battleship and performed outstanding work directing repairs and rescuing the wounded."

LIEUTENANT (jg) J.D. PARKER, U.S. NAVY

"For showing extraordinary courage and disregard for his own safety. As senior officer present on the drydocked destroyer **USS DOWNES,** he handled the emergency in a 'most outstanding manner' although wounded."

RADIOMAN FIRST CLASS C.W. PERRY, U.S. NAVY

"For showing extraordinary courage and disregard of his own safety. He first attempted to man an aircraft machine gun under heavy fire at Naval Air Station, Kaneohe; then took a mortally wounded Ensign in a truck to the dispensary under heavy enemy strafing; and finally returned to help salvage planes under fire."

RADIOMAN SECOND CLASS J.G. RAINES, U.S. NAVY

"For showing extraordinary courage and disregard of his own safety. Along with Radioman First Class R.E. Jones, he rescued one man and tried to save another trapped in a flame and smoke filled transmitter room on a patrol plane tender."

*COXSWAIN E.T. READER, U.S. NAVY

"For showing extraordinary courage and disregard of his own safety. As an antiaircraft gun captain, he fought his own weapon in local control, despite heavy casualties in his crew, exploding ammunition on deck and serious fires, until killed at his station."

COMMANDER D.G.J. SHEA, U.S. NAVY

"For showing extraordinary courage and disregard of his own safety. As commanding officer of the drydocked destroyer **USS CASSIN,** he directed flooding of the dock, fighting fires and abandoning his ship without loss of personnel under heavy bombing."

*SIMENSEN, CARLETON E., SECOND LIEUTENANT, U.S.M.C.

"For heroic leadership and devotion to duty during the attack on the U.S. Pacific Fleet in Pearl Harbor, T.H., by Japanese forces on December 7, 1941. During the first few moments of the attack on the **USS ARIZONA,** he led the Marines up the exposed ladders of the mainmast in spite of the heavy bombing and strafing attack. Upon reaching the searchlight platform he was mortally wounded. He died almost instantly but not before he motioned to the Marine personnel not to assist him but to continue to their battle stations in secondary aft. His courage and gallant leadership are an inspiration to all."

NOTE: This Letter of Commendation was later upgraded to a Bronze Star with Combat "V".

*BOATSWAIN MATE FIRST CLASS A. SOLAR, U.S. NAVY

"For showing extraordinary courage and disregard of his own safety in opening fire early against the enemy and controlling his gun in an outstanding manner until killed by shell fragments on board the battleship **USS NEVADA.**"

ENSIGN R.L. STEWARD, U.S. NAVY

"For showing extraordinary courage and disregard of his own safety. On the **USS DOWNES,** he fought available antiaircraft machine guns until forced to jump to safety, despite a broken foot; and afterwards he helped hospitalize the wounded."

AVIATION ORDNANCEMAN SECOND CLASS E.L. WENTZLAFF, U.S. NAVY

"For showing extraordinary courage and disregard of his own safety, when he began damage control preparations before general quarters sounded on the **USS ARIZONA,** and after she had been badly bombed, obtained the admiral's barge, in which he rescued wounded in oil-fire waters."

THE FREEDOM OF INFORMATION ACT

THE FREEDOM OF INFORMATION ACT prevents access to information regarding living recipients. Unless the information was previously published and therefore in the public domain, it has often been exceedingly difficult or impossible to obtain the complete details we would like to present in this volume.

ACKNOWLEDGMENTS

We are grateful to the following individuals and Commands who cooperated by researching and sharing information with us to complete and authenticate this study. The production of this book was possible only with their interest and cooperation.

Leatrice R. Arakahi, Historian, Department of the Air Force, Headquarters 15th Air Base Wing, Hickam Air Force Base, Hawaii

Army Awards Branch Headquarters, Department of the Army, Alexandria, Virginia

Stanley J. Barnett, Chief of Office of Pacific Air Force History, Hickam Air Force Base, Hawaii

General Robert H. Barrow, Commandant U.S. Marine Corps, Washington, D.C.

Biographical Records, U.S. Navy Department, Washington, DC

Captain William S. Busik, USN (Ret.) Executive Director, U.S. Naval Academy Alumni Association, Annapolis, Maryland

Ray Collins, historical researcher, Alexandria, Virginia

Danny J. Crawford, Head Reference Section, History and Museums Division, Headquarters U.S. Marine Corps, Washington, DC

Department of the Air Force, Headquarters Pacific Air Force, Hickam Air Force Base, Hawaii

Department of Army Historical Reference Branch, Military History and Center of Military History, Washington, DC

Technical Sergeant Jack O. Ehrke, Supply Sergeant, 19th Transport Squadron, Hickam Field in 1941

Thomas M. Fairfull, Museum Director, U.S. Army, Fort Shafter, Hawaii

Paul D. Gray, Assistant Director Military Records, National Personnel Records Center, St. Louis, Missouri

Gerald E. Hasselwander, Deputy Chief, Research Division, Maxwell Air Force Base, Alabama

Bruce Headley, Director Museum Fort Lewis, Washington

History and Museums Division, Headquarters, U.S. Marine Corps, Washington, DC

Headquarters U.S. Marine Corps, Department of the Navy, Washington, DC

Headquarters U.S. Army Support Command, Hawaii, Fort Shafter, Hawaii

Honolulu State Library Microfilm Services, Honolulu, Hawaii

S.J. (Jeanne) Kirk, Head Awards and Special Projects Branch, Department of Navy, Washington, DC

John Lewis, Medal Collector, Sheriff's Department, Yakima WA

McChord Air Force Base Library, McChord Air Force Base, Washington

Naval Historical Center, Department of the Navy, Washington, DC

News Releases, U.S. Navy Department, Washington, DC

Office of the Chief of Naval operations, Washington, DC

Mrs. Margaret Ono, Base Librarian, McChord Air Force Base, Washington State

Brigadier General E.H. Simons, USMC (Ret.) Director Marine Corps History and Museums, Washington, DC

Sinclair Graduate Library Micro-film Facilities, University of Hawaii, Honolulu, Hawaii

Captain M.B. Sousa, U.S. Navy, Deputy Director Naval History, Washington Navy Yard, Washington, DC

Betty Sprigg, Office of Secretary of Defense, Pentagon, Washington, DC

Colonel E.G. Taylor, General Staff, Chief of Staff, 24th Infantry Division, (Mechanized) and Fort Stewart, Georgia

Chief Warrant Officer W.B. Thayer, U.S. Army, Military Awards Branch, Alexandria, Virginia

U.S. Naval Academy Alumni Association, Annapolis, Maryland

Colonel Robert E. Waggoner, Chief, Historical Services Division, Washington, DC

Dr. Timothy Warnock, Researcher, Headquarters Albert F. Simpson Air Historical Research Center, Maxwell Air Force Base, Alabama

Charles E. Young, civilian at Hickam Field, (T.H.) 1941

Colonel J.B. Egan, Commanding Officer, U.S. Marine Corps Barracks, Bangor Submarine Base, Bremerton, Washington

Sergeant Daniel Hoffman, U.S.M.C. Photographer, Bangor Sub Base, Bremerton, Washington

Major Henry J. Romero, AUS (Ret.) Retirement Services Officer, Dept. of the Army, HQI Corps and Fort Lewis, Fort Lewis, WA

BIBLIOGRAPHY

BOOKS

Bunkley, J.W., MILITARY AND NAVAL RECOGNITION BOOK, New York, New York, 1941

Clark, Blake, REMEMBER PEARL HARBOR, New York, New York, Harper, 1943

Editors of ARMY TIMES, PEARL HARBOR AND HAWAII, New York, New York, Walker and Company, 1971

Editors of Boston Publishing Company, ABOVE AND BEYOND, a TIME-LIFE Book, Boston, Massachusetts, 1985

Holbrook, Stuart, NONE MORE COURAGEOUS, New York, New York, Macmillan, 1942

Karig, Cdr. Walter, USNR and Kelley, Lt. Welbourn, USNR, BATTLE REPORT, New York, New York, Farrar & Rhinehart, 1944

Lambert, John W., THE LONG CAMPAIGN, Manhattan, Kansas, Sunflower University Press, 1982

Navy Department, MEDAL OF HONOR, 1861-1949, THE NAVY (Special Printing) Gov't. Printing, Washington, DC, 1949

Robles, Philip K., UNITED STATES MILITARY MEDALS & RIBBONS, Rutland, Vermont, Tokyo, Japan, Charles E. Tuttle Co., 1971

Ross, Donald K. & Helen L., WASHINGTON STATE MEN OF VALOR, Burley, Washington, Coffee Break Press, 1980

USAF Historical Study No. 85, USAF CREDITS FOR THE DESTRUCTION OF ENEMY AIRCRAFT, WW II, Office of Air Force History, USAF, Washington, DC, 1978

U.S.S. NEVADA (Yearbook), San Francisco, California, The James H. Barry Company, 1946

U.S. Senate, MEDAL OF HONOR RECIPIENTS, 1861-1978, Washington, DC, Government Printing, 1978

MAGAZINES

LIFE Magazines, New York, New York
PARADISE OF THE PACIFIC, San Francisco, California
TIME Magazines, New York, New York

NEWSLETTERS

Congressional Medal of Honor Society Newsletter, Elma, Washington
Medal of Honor Historical Round Table, Philadelphia, Pennsylvania

Medal of Honor Historical Society, Lombard, Illinois

Pearl Harbor Gram, Lancaster, California

NEWSPAPERS of December 1941 through June 1942

CHICAGO TRIBUNE, Chicago, Illinois

HONOLULU ADVERTISER, Honolulu, Territory of Hawaii

HONOLULU STAR-BULLETIN, Honolulu, Territory of Hawaii

KANSAS CITY STAR, Kansas City, Missouri

LONG BEACH PRESS-TELEGRAM, Long Beach, California

OFFICIAL PAPERS

BuPers, Navy, Public Information, NAV 328, Citations of March 2-18, 1942

National Personnel Records Center, St. Louis, Missouri

Navy Department of Press Relations, June 9, 1942 and September 24, 1942

Navy Office of Information, Biographies Branch, Internal Relations, Division (01-430) 9 April 1962 and 15 March 1962

Office of PACAF History, Department of Air Force, HQ Pacific Air Forces, Hickam AFB, Hawaii

Research Division, HQ Albert F. Simpson Historical Research Center, Maxwell AFB, Alabama

U.S. Army General Orders No. 2, War Department, January 5, 1942

INDEX